Crosscurrents/MODERN CRITIQUES

Crosscurrents/MODERN CRITIQUES

Harry T. Moore, *General Editor*

CHRISTOPHER FRY

Emil Roy

WITH A PREFACE BY

Harry T. Moore

Carbondale and Edwardsville

SOUTHERN ILLINOIS UNIVERSITY PRESS

FEFFER & SIMONS, INC.

London and Amsterdam

Preface

In many cultures there was no prose drama; the actors in the theater spoke only poetry. The first great dramatic writers, the Athenians, expressed themselves in verse, and so did the playwrights who re-created the drama in Europe about a thousand years later.

By the time we get to Shakespeare, the dramatists are putting various passages into prose. That tremendous comic figure, Falstaff, is essentially a man of prose, but even Hamlet can speak in that medium, whether in the enraptured "What a piece of work is a man!" or in the amusing exchange with the gravedigger.

After the Restoration in England, there were still poetic dramas, notably the heroic plays in blank verse, but the comic authors, seeking realism, wrote their comedies in prose. Similarly, in the eighteenth century, Sheridan and Goldsmith turned out comedies in prose. In the Romantic period, however, Shelley, Keats, and Byron all wrote poetic tragedies. These remain read rather than produced, though in The Death of Tragedy (1961) George Steiner made out an excellent case for Byron's plays as dramatically viable.

Meanwhile in France the poetic drama had been kept up in the seventeenth century by Corneille and Racine, and in Germany in the eighteenth by Goethe and Schiller. The most important dramatist of the nineteenth century, Henrik Ibsen, began as a writer of verse drama but switched over in 1871, with Emperor and Galilean. Although this was a historical play, Ibsen said that he was

living in an age of realism and that he would write in
that vein. He continued it in his plays with modern settings. "But," as Edmund Wilson notes in Axel's Castle,
"in the later prose plays of Ibsen, the trolls and ghosts
of his early dramatic poems have begun to creep back into
the bourgeois drawing-rooms . . . All that vaporous, confused and grandiose world of Romanticism had been
resolutely ordered and compressed; but now the objective
point of view of Naturalism, the machine-like technique
that went with it, began to cramp the poet's imagination,
to prove inadequate to convey what he feels. The reader
begins to chafe at the strain, and the artist begins to betray
it." It is true that Ibsen's concepts became poetic again
(The Wild Duck, The Master Builder), but his language
remained prose.

Late in Ibsen's career, at the end of the nineteenth
century, an Englishman dared revive poetic drama. This
was Stephen Phillips, with his Paolo and Francesca
(1899), Herod (1900), and Ulysses (1902), which were
highly successful on the London stage; then the vogue for
Phillips went out suddenly, and few authors attempted
plays in verse. T. S. Eliot was interested in such dramas,
however, and around the time of the First World War
wrote several essays about the possibilities of a new poetic
drama in those years before he ventured into the area himself. The success of his plays is well known, from Murder
in the Cathedral to The Cocktail Party and The Con-
fidential Clerk. But Eliot uses a special range of versifica-
tion, not too strongly rhythmical and in no way anti-
quated. After he had found himself as a man of the
theater, Eliot noted that verse in a play must be more than
ornamental: "It must justify itself dramatically, and not
merely be fine poetry shaped into dramatic form."

Others besides Eliot were trying poetic drama, among
them Christopher Fry, the subject of the present book.
Its author has made a devotedly careful study of this playwright, who first really crossed my own consciousness a
few years after the Second World War when, in Boston,
I saw The Lady's not for Burning. The production fea-

tured John Gielgud and Pamela Brown and introduced a bright young actor named Richard Burton. It was a pleasure to hear poetry, a poetry alive with sharpness, spoken in the theater.

Since his first geniune successes, Christopher Fry has had a mixed time of it, which can be traced through this book. It is a useful volume about the modern theater, useful because it makes a valuable investigation of Fry without overrating him. Emil Roy in this study shows how fine a man of the theater Fry is, a writer of illuminating dialogue and the creator of characters who confront some of the salient issues of our time.

Mr. Roy examines Fry's themes at length and makes pertinent comments on them; fortunately he does not keep his book merely thematic and conceptual but also makes technical observations of value.

It is too early to attempt to place Christopher Fry, to assess what his position will be in the far future; but Mr. Roy has given us a good and lively book for today and one that may contribute toward the ultimate placing of its subject.

HARRY T. MOORE

Southern Illinois University
April 18, 1968

Contents

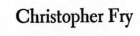

Christopher Fry

1

Outlook and Ideas

A full measure of critical recognition first came to Christopher Fry with the production of *The Lady's not for Burning* at London's Arts Theatre Club, March 20, 1948. The play won the Shaw prize for best play of the year, toured the provinces for eight weeks and then reopened at the Globe, London. There it achieved an enormous popular success which was soon repeated on the other side of the Atlantic. Fry had not been previously unknown. With more practical experience in the theater than any other modern English playwright since Bernard Shaw, Fry had seen three of his religious plays produced before the war and one of them published, *The Boy with a Cart*, in 1939. After the war his religious tragedy, *The Firstborn*, was published in 1946 and broadcast by the B.B.C. in 1947, while *A Phoenix too Frequent*, a one-acter considered his best play by many critics, was successfully produced in 1946. But *The Lady* marked the beginning of a furious outburst of creative energy which resulted in the first productions of six original plays and three translations (from the French) in the next eight years.

The reviewers in the daily press were ecstatic in their praise of Fry as a contemporary Shakespeare. The academics also saw the parallels, but found them more to Fry's discredit. He had either slavishly imitated the weaker plays or the superficial traits of Shakespeare, they felt, or he had utilized stage conventions which were outmoded or inappropriate: the Elizabethan wit-combats, bombast, passages of exuberant invective and wordplay. (That Sean

O'Casey and, to a lesser extent, Bernard Shaw had also done so was usually overlooked. Their use more recently by such dramatists as John Osborne, Harold Pinter and Edward Albee suggests that the brisk use of rhetoric for its own sake on the stage has yet to run dry.) The "rather soggy" contemporary audience would laugh at them indulgently, the more sceptical critics felt, having brought to the theater the expectations they would normally bring to a revival of Shakespeare. Critics were also quick to find his verse distractingly autonomous, self-consciously literary and often marred by joking wordplays. His characters all spoke very much alike, it was complained. Marius Bewley summed up the position of his detractors with a much-quoted aphorism: for him Fry applied a grand style to trivial themes, "what one might expect of *Paradise Lost* if it were rewritten by Ogden Nash." [1]

Yet in one of the best essays ever written on Fry, Monroe Spears recognized that Fry was better at dramatic verse than any recent writer except Eliot: his language was alive and contemporary, heightened into genuine poetry and usually well-calculated for speaking. Another fine critic, the classical scholar Martin Arrowsmith turned for resemblances away from Shakespeare to his earlier contemporary, Marlowe. This, he commented,

> says something about the texture of Fry's drama, if not of his verse: there is the same verbal impatience, the laddering of effects toward an over-all tonal roof, and the exuberance and extravagance of the autonomous language which is only an extension of the theme itself.[2]

Fry's language was flamboyant and pulsive, finessing its mystery by a verbal bravura and high rhetoric that is rare in modern poetry, he concluded. Although Fry has repeatedly stressed his reluctance to engage in critical controversies over his plays, he struck back hard at the image of himself which some reviewers had presented.

> *The Lady's not for Burning*, the play which first gave rise to the bacchic figure vomiting his careless words, was five or six months finding its shape before writing began, and eight

months in writing. I don't mean that slowness in writing is a virtue: it is an incapacity; but it's hard to relate it to verbal intoxication; it feels more like a slow death by ground glass.[3]

Fry's place in the contemporary theater, both inside and outside T. S. Eliot's poetic drama movement, was just as hotly debated as his supposed indebtedness to the Elizabethans, the Restoration wits and—nearer our own time—the stillborn Victorian and Edwardian verse dramatists. While Donoghue drew disparaging comparisons between his plays and those of such nonentities as Masefield and Bottomley, Raymond Williams thought that Fry's masters in comedy were not Jonson or Massinger, nor the Synge of *Playboy*, but Oscar Wilde, Shaw, Chekhov, and indirectly, Pirandello. Although Fry's plays fall into two neat groups, his religious plays and his comedies, Williams found only tenuous links between his work and the drama of Yeats and Eliot. Arrowsmith, however, stressed the debt of a whole group of playwrights to Eliot, finding hardly a verse dramatist of talent who did not derive from Eliot's determination to have a verse drama. Eliot's notes connecting the form of ballet and drama were taken up by Auden and Isherwood, Arrowsmith believed (although Yeats had arrived at the same idea years earlier with the help of Ezra Pound's Noh drama). And from Eliot's notes on dramatic liturgy were derived Anne Ridler's nativity play, *The Shadow Factory*, Ronald Duncan's masque and anti-masque, *This Way to the Tomb*, as well as Fry's two festival plays, *The Boy with a Cart* and *Thor, with Angels*. Of the entire group, Arrowsmith believes, only Fry and perhaps Auden managed to shake off Eliot's stylistic hold. And it was by looking to the example of Charles Williams and before Williams, to Beddoes, Arrowsmith concluded, that Fry managed to strike out on his own.

Fry's outlook and ideas have been no less controversial. He is an apparent follower of Eliot against whom Eliot's most stringent dicta have been applied, a lover of homeland among wanderers, a serious writer of frivolous comedies, and (to some) an eschatological and irreverent composer of religious plays. A moderate in religious and political outlook, he is as witty, urbane, and rhetorically brilliant as his existentialist French contemporaries. While attacking Sartre's theories, Fry has gone on to translate five plays by Anouilh and Giraudoux. And although Fry has always been a Christian, the working out of his faith in his plays has often appeared so unsystematic and even ambiguous that Bonamy Dobrée has termed him a "Christian agnostic."

Three influential factors emerge from Fry's early life: a religious family background, an education emphasizing both the literary and performing arts, and a love of provincial nature. Fry never went to Paris or America as a voluntary exile, although he occasionally travels on the Continent and in the United States. No matter where or when his plays are set, Fry shows the keenest interest in flora, fauna, and cosmic phenomena. Derek Stanford has placed him "midway between Wordsworth's nature-philosophy and Keats's sensuous appreciation." [4] Nor has Fry ever broken with the religious and moral traditions inherited from his parents, although he has shown a far keener awareness of moral and social disorder than the Edwardians ever sensed.

Fry was born on December 18, 1907, at Bristol, in the West Country. He was the younger son of Charles John Harris, who had begun his career as an architect. Although his father failed to prosper at first, just when things began looking up he gave up his practice and became an Anglican lay-preacher and mission-worker for St. Agnes parish in the Bristol slums. "He was what was then called a Christian socialist, or something very like it," Fry recalls. His enthusiasm was enormous, but he carried a heavy burden. Stanford has recounted that he would return home late in the evening, only to leave again taking his waiting dinner to some needy family. In 1910, his health ruined, he died.

Christopher was three when his father died. Along with a brother, who was six years older, he was brought up in

Bedford by his mother with the help of an aunt, both of them religious women. His aunt read aloud to him from *Pilgrim's Progress,* and Fry has ever since referred to Bedford as "Bunyan's town." At about the same time his budding musical and theatrical talents were encouraged and stimulated. Fry had begun to play the piano as a young child. At the age of five he composed a "Pharaoh's March" and appeared on stage in a civic pageant when he was six. Fry has recalled that he was particularly interested in "what were called accidentals—those notes of chromatic alteration which made all the difference to the simple notes of the octave." He even invented a piece for the piano called "The Lovers' Quarrel," which was, he thought, entirely composed of accidentals.

> And I was always very taken with the unexpected notes which occurred in a melody, or in a chord—notes I would never have anticipated, which nevertheless took their perfect place in the general harmony, as though they had flown in like birds and woken the whole landscape into receiving them.

Fry's mother was the former Emma Marguerite Hammond ("it was her mother who was a Fry"). She took in boarders to send Christopher to the Bedford Modern School, which had a reputation as one of the best of its kind. Fry earned no distinction in his formal English studies, or in any of the other parts of his education, for that matter.

> I remember myself at the age of ten or eleven being mildly interested in some of it, though some things about it seemed very eccentric. An extraordinary amount of fuss was made about triangles, for instance, though so far as I could see, triangles hardly occurred in the world at all. . . . So there were times when my attention wandered. . . . I hadn't seen that . . . education—a word that means a leading out—would lead me out beyond anything I could have dreamed of.

Yet Fry began writing early in adolescence, producing a farce at eleven, a poem at twelve, and at the age of fourteen, an unacted and unpublished verse drama. The play, *Youth and Peregrines*, written when he was seventeen, was finally produced in 1934, when he was director of the Wells Repertory Players at Tunbridge Wells. Interestingly enough, it appeared on a bill that included the world premier of Shaw's *Village Wooing*, which Fry had obtained for his company.

When he left school at eighteen, however, a year after writing this play, he changed his name.

> I took the name Fry by deed-poll [on his own] when I started working in the theatre: largely because at the time I knew the Fry part of the family more intimately than my father's side; and was much helped and encouraged by my mother's cousin John Fry and his wife Nancy (to whom I dedicated *Curtmantle*).

During the next year he acted as master at the Hazelwood Preparatory School in Limpsfield, Surrey, and tutored the nephew of Lord Ampthill. Sometime during the same year, while he was "a callow nineteen," Fry met a poet for the first time. He was W. H. Davies, who was then fifty-six, nearly forty years Fry's senior, now remembered mostly for his anthology pieces, "Sleep" and "Leisure." The latter poem ends as it proceeds, rather banally, with "A poor life this if, full of care, / We have no time to stand and stare." Fry recalls,

> I was prepared to leave my shoes at the door and go in barefooted. But Davies talked throughout the evening about the internal combustion engine, of which he knew very little, though it seemed he had a tenacious interest in it. And on our second meeting, when we were alone together, he talked for an hour and twenty minutes about drains.

Fry then left teaching in 1927 to become an actor, joining the Citizen House, Bath, which was both a social center and a theater. But he was forced by the inherent instability of the profession back to teaching again at Limpsfield, this time for three years. After he had managed to save £10, he left teaching for good. Fry has recalled this discouraging period in his dedication of *A Sleep of Prisoners* (1951) to Robert Gittings. Intent on making Fry write, Gittings had invited him for a summer holiday in 1931 to an old deserted Somerset rectory, Thorn St. Margaret. Gittings, a longtime friend, poet, and frequent defender of Fry's plays, has since also written verse drama containing unmistakable echoes of Fry's ideas and metaphors. As he remembers, Fry had written nothing for five or six years, and was to write almost nothing again for five years following. Yet that summer, sustained by a barrel of beer and a crate of biscuits, they both sat down to write. Fry has recalled,

> The ten years in which you loyally thought of me as a writer when clearly I wasn't, your lectures to me on my self-defensive mockery of artists, and those two leisurely months under the Quantocks, were things of friendship which kept me in a proper mind.

The result of Fry's labors was the still-unacted, unpublished comedy *Siege*. Writing this play convinced him "that one day the words would come."

For the next eight years Fry was to make a stubborn living from repertory troupes, acting the usual rounds of Shakespeare, Shaw, Wilde, Barrie, and Coward. Like a number of eventually successful dramatists, he was forced to subsist on a series of odd jobs, although he was more fortunate than most in finding positions connected with the stage. After working for a while as secretary to a popular song writer, he tried his hand as a cabaret entertainer. He also edited a magazine, tried cartooning, and worked as secretary to a novelist.

In 1934 Fry joined the Repertory Players at Tunbridge Wells where he both acted and directed until the enterprise failed. His most notable acting assignment was male lead in Shaw's *A Village Wooing*. During the same period Fry wrote music and lyrics for an André Charlot revue. He also did *She Shall Have Music*, a standard musical about a crooner which enjoyed a brief run at the Saville Theatre in London. "I wanted to find out about the theatre," Fry has said. "It was also mainly accidental." The musical was also acted with various groups and directed at the Oxford Playhouse both immediately before and after the war. Fry once told a reporter that he writes "an occasional parody of the classics such as his version of *Macbeth* in which the three witches are girl reporters." In 1951 he composed the music, which Leslie Bridgewater scored for him, for Peter Brooks's production of Shakespeare's *A Winter's Tale*. And in 1953 he wrote extra lyrics for the film of John Gay's *The Beggar's Opera*.

Of the years from 1935 to 1939 Fry told *Who's Who* his life was "too complicated for tabulation." Up to 1939, although he had written several plays which had been performed at rather special occasions, Fry had had none of his dramas published. He had written a play on the life of Thomas Barnardo, the founder of Dr. Barnardo's Homes, a charitable organization caring for orphaned and abandoned children. With this play, *Open Door*, he toured England for two years, from late 1934 to 1936, acting and lecturing. Soon afterwards, in 1937, he wrote *The Boy with a Cart* for a local rector; the play was also acted by village groups and served to introduce Fry to the Religious Drama Society and its president, the Bishop of Chichester. Two years later it was published.

Fry has always been a careful, painstaking writer. He began work on *The Firstborn* in 1938: twenty years later he was still revising it. Although Stanford reported *Curtmantle* in progress as early as 1950 or 1951, Fry says it was started later, in 1957, or late in 1956 at the earliest, and was interrupted by a year of film writing in Italy. However, the play was not produced until 1961. "The time the plays took to write varied considerably," Fry comments, "*Phoenix*, three months; *Thor with Angels* not more than five weeks; *The Lady*, nine months; *Sleep of Prisoners*, six months; *The Dark* about eighteen months, I think."

In 1936 Fry married Phyllis Hart, the journalist, and finished *The Boy with a Cart* the next year. By 1938 "there was no money at all," but fortunately he was left a small legacy by a cousin. In the meantime two of his pageants were written and produced. He finished *The Tower* in 1939. According to Stanford it shows the influence of Eliot's pageant *The Rock*, presented as a benefit at the Sadler's Wells Theater five years before. The *Times* of London reported that *The Tower* was

> an attractively youthful piece of work. It sets out to recount the history of the Abbey in terms of the spiritual conflict between pride and humility; but so interested in ideas is the author that we are left in the end with no very vivid impression of history, but with the agreeable sensation of having overheard a terrific argument on the nature of man.

Fry also wrote a similar pageant called *Thursday's Child*, which was produced at Albert Hall and attended by Queen Mary. Neither play, however, has been published. The same year (1939) Fry became director of the Oxford Playhouse, where he met the young actress Pamela Brown, for whom he later wrote *The Lady's not for Burning*. After a few months Fry, a conscientious objector, was called up and assigned to a noncombatant arm of the Forces. He served for four years with the Pioneer Corps, taking part in clearing away bomb damage and helping fight blitz fires at the Liverpool docks in 1941. In 1944, however, Fry's health apparently broke down. He was hospitalized and then mustered out in the late summer. Fry then returned to the Arts Theatre Club in London as resident playwright after doing two productions there, *The School for Scandal* and *The Circle of Chalk*. This led directly to *A Phoenix too Frequent* in 1946 and his full-blown career as writer and translator which followed. "A man's work is what his life is," Fry has written, "and he can only grow where he seeks."

In his youth Fry was assimilating the Bible, Bunyan, Shakespeare, the Greek and Roman myths, and Malory. In school the influences of Sir Thomas Browne, Bergson's *Creative Evolution* and Wordsworth were significant. Later in the theater he encountered Chekhov, Shaw, Wilde, and Ibsen, although he had some difficulty with Congreve's *The Way of the World* "where plot is an infernal nuisance, so huddled together to be out of the way of the true comedy that it took me hours to work it out before I produced it at Oxford." Later came Eliot and then Rilke in J. B. Leishman's translation. But any listing is bound to be partial, as Fry has indicated in a letter: "most of this is a guess. We are like jackdaws: we catch at bright objects everywhere."

Fry's style is predominantly witty, metaphorically opulent, and hyperbolic. Although he had experimented with several types of intricate rhythmic and stanzaic patterns in his early *Boy*, his postwar production has relied mainly on irregular blank verse and prose, except for an occasional song. His audacious, sometimes strained metaphors are especially noticeable in all his plays up to the latest in time of conception, *The Dark is Light Enough* (1954). And despite his studied aloofness from the critical wars, attacks on his idiom have drawn him repeatedly to the defense. He has "meant the ornament to be, dramatically or comedically, an essential part of the meaning." And again, he has replied somewhat acidly in describing the picture of himself which has emerged from press clippings.

> I see a man reeling intoxicated with words: they flow in a golden—or perhaps pinchbeck—stream from his mouth: they start out at his ears; they burst like rockets and jumping crackers and catherine-wheels round his head; they spring in wanton sport at his feet and trip him; but trip him or not, he loves them: let them all come, go where they may; let them strangle sense, flood the stage, break the dams of form: facility shall have its day.[5]

The texture of Fry's language is far more opencast, like Spenser's or Marlowe's, than contemporary canons of criticism can accept, focused as they are on tightly-knit ambiguity and layers of meaning. His symbolism and imagery are certainly open to explication. But as Arrowsmith points out, Fry's type of language must take to some kind of self-mockery: it likes to cancel out or qualify its own explicit exorbitance. This is done either with fantastic whimsy or with a prosy counter-voice. We often feel about

Fry's wit as Eric Bentley has described Oscar Wilde's: that the endemic quibbling and apparently irresponsible wordplays are actually a pseudo-irresponsible jabbing at all great problems. Hence his style has both an accumulative and paradoxical effect. As with the Restoration comic dramatists, his wit involves the ability not only to perceive the incongruities of human behavior and thought but to be master of them in a playful manner.

On occasion Fry's language is strained and straining, precious and even banal. But these affectations drop away as the verse in his later plays become increasingly spare and proselike. One of his most characteristic traits is the repetition of words and phrases by or between characters to convey a sense of inner tension, as in *Thor, with Angels*: "Who at it? Not you at it. Don't you / Think he's ever at it. Nobody's at it." And throughout his work aphorisms and truisms appear. However, Fry avoids oversimplification by reversing part of a phrase, as when Perpetua in *Venus Observed* had been found "unsafe for democracy," creating an ironic discrepancy between what is expected and what is actually said. And there is the O'Casey-like abandon of invective: "crimping, constipated duffer . . . You spigoted, bigoted, operculated prig," all of these traits meant to reveal the paradoxical enfolding of the practical within the miraculous, the divine in the temporal.

Fry seems to conceive each of his plays as a poem of quasi-lyrical feeling which is developed and explored dramatically. But by referring to his nonreligious plays as "comedies," he has unavoidably misled his critics. His romanticized settings, paired sentimental lovers, skill in vituperation, innocent heroines and seasonal moods link him to the Shakespeare of *Much Ado About Nothing, A Midsummer Night's Dream,* and *Twelfth Night,* along with countless comedies written since. Yet all of his plays properly belong to the tradition of tragicomedy, a form which has also been called "problem play," "dark comedy," or Suzanne Langer's "averted tragedy." Historically, tragicomedy has had its fullest expression in the last sixty years, but it also appeared in Athens' declining years, in England at the end of the sixteenth and early seventeenth centuries, in Moliere's France under Louis XIV and in Russia at the end of the nineteenth century. Nearly all contemporary masterpieces have been written in his vein, including Ibsen's *The Wild Duck,* Chekhov's *The Cherry Orchard,* Shaw's *Saint Joan,* Pirandello's *Henry IV* and *Six Characters,* Beckett's *Waiting for Godot* and Ionesco's *The Chairs,* to make only a partial listing.

The starting point of Fry's theater involves some of the basic elements of drama, the suspense created by pure, preliterary theater: a poetic image, a mood or atmosphere, and a theme. He has claimed that he has never set to work until he has seen the whole shape and conclusion of a play. With these intuitive, almost nonverbal elements in mind Fry presses his action forward from an anecdotal, often audacious situation, adjusting the relationships among his characters in terms of atmosphere or mood. "I don't know whether a comedy of mood is an accepted category," he has written, "or whether it's something I've coined to cover my particular end. It means that the scene, the season and the characters are bound together in one climate." [6] As a result, comedy merges with tragedy, farce with romance. Even flat, stock types use an extraordinarily rich, metaphorical language, and the realistic, even threatening plot is contrasted with a plethora of nonrealistic devices such as involved symbolism, *coups de theatre,* songs, transformations, and illuminations. In his book on *Modern Tragicomedy* Karl Guthke has concluded that the light of Fry's comedies is

> visible only because of the underlying darkness of tragedy that it is focused on, arousing as it does that strange twilight of pensive melancholy mixed with barely subdued joy that is the hallmark of Fry's art.[7]

If as Bentley suggests, the two most successful types of tragicomedy are tragedy with a happy ending and comedy with an unhappy ending, Fry writes the former, as he has explained in his important essay on "Comedy."

I know that when I set about writing a comedy the idea presents itself to me first of all as tragedy. The characters press on to the theme with all their divisions and perplexities heavy about them; they are already entered for the race to doom, and good and evil are an infernal tangle skinning the fingers that try to unravel them. . . . Somehow the characters have to unmortify themselves; to affirm life and assimilate death and persevere in joy.[8]

All of Fry's plays reveal this progression. A death occurs at the end of most of his religious plays and *The Dark is Light Enough*, while the comedies, *The Boy* and *A Sleep of Prisoners* approach and recede from what Northrop Frye calls "the point of ritual death." However, except for *The Dark* it is a minor character who dies. Only in *Thor, with Angels* is it premeditated murder. And in all the plays a central character makes his "narrow escape into faith."

What distinguishes Fry's comedies from his religious plays, however, is the kind of sustained tension between character and mood. In the religious plays, essentially comic persons, who may be capable of the tragic by virtue of their complexity and depth, find themselves in the world of tragedy. In *The Firstborn*, *A Sleep of Prisoners*, and *Thor, with Angels* the protagonist may escape the catastrophic destruction which overthrows the old order, but at the cost of an atoning death of one who dies from him. While the victim enlightens the protagonist to the full extent of his blessing, the victor affirms the redemption which awaits the survivors of the victim's tragically disordered society.

In the "comedies," however, a character fit for tragedy is contrasted with a world which belongs to comedy. Into societies preoccupied with zoning laws, mundane routines of prayer, marriage festivals, and urbane logic-chopping intrudes a guilt-ridden, death-seeker. Furtively aware of her wifely shortcomings, Dynamene in *A Phoenix* seeks to join the dead Virilius, and Thomas Mendip in *The Lady* tries to trick the Mayor of Cool Clary into hanging him to expiate his real guilt, ostensibly for murder but actually for deaths he had unavoidably dealt as a soldier. The Duke of Altair in *Venus Observed* wants to remarry. Once engaged in a passionate saturnalia of ecstasy with his first wife, he lost her and wants to dull old sorrows. And Richard Gettner in *The Dark, poète maudit,* deserter and drunkard, hopes for the cessation of all painful sensation. All around them, however, nature bursts into growth or color, couples fall in love at first sight, and society celebrates rebirth with festival, joviality and merrymaking. Dynamene's over-sexed maid, the pompous Mayor with his cold, the Duke's thieving, culture-loving agent, and the high-spirited soldiers who occupy the Countess Rosmarin's house are all Bergsonian: something mechanical encrusted on the living.

Another familiar tragicomic device involves the linking of two plots of equal weight, one which is tragic, the other comic, with a similar theme and comparable motifs in both. Fry often uses the technique as a subordinate device, paralleling the increasingly ill-fraught love of protagonists with the romantic passions of a minor couple. Richard and Alizon, Perpetua and the inconspicuous Edgar, Peter and Gelda love blindly and unconsciously, but their affairs are relatively unimportant in the action. Only in *Thor, with Angels* is a double plot sustained in balance throughout the whole duration of the play: disastrous romance and romantic salvation blend throughout, but the play is Fry's weakest.

However, tragicomedy at its best depends not on the juxtaposition of comic and tragic, but upon a subtle integration. As J. L. Styan has put it, the dark comedian must make the audience suffer without the relief of tears, and make it mock without the relief of laughter. The audience remains at a distance, yet within immediate call; impersonal, yet strangely involved. "It is a world of its own," Fry has said in *An Experience of Critics,* "but not a world all of one kind." It is not that Fry is not funny. He often is. "A joke, even a bad one, can reflect the astonishing light we live in," he has said, and in *The Lady* Mendip remarks, "laughter, madam, is an irrelevance that almost

amounts to revelation." But in "Comedy" Fry rejects the
view that man could, "in his first unlaughing condition,
have contrived a comic view of life and then developed
the strange rib-shaking response." He is more interested in
laughter as the titillation of the mind rather than as the
Lockean perception of superiority; it is the reawakening of
forgotten intuitions. As a result he must reach comedy by
way of tragedy. "In a century less flayed and quivering we
might reach it more directly; but not now, unless every
word we write is going to mock us." Despite his rejection
of the theater of naturalism, which presents life as a vision
of unmitigated horror, Fry is just as aware as O'Casey,
Brecht and O'Neill that contrariety is at the heart of the
universe. His plays reflect the breakdown in contemporary
values, and his awareness of the loss of stable, implicitly
accepted social standards emerges in his longing for a fresh
start with the center of unity restored.

> We should really take ourselves back to the creation of the
> world, and watch chaos inspired with form, the multiplicity
> of shape, rhythm, pattern, texture, kind, expounded with
> one creative impulse.

The outer world of events gives way to the inner world of
perception when the character can say with Dante as he
addresses God, "Thy will is our peace." Man must make
his way "by the difficult experience of tragedy and the
intuition of comedy."

With Pirandello and Anouilh, Fry has found it necessary to invent a fairy-tale world of make-believe to win our
consent to his ideas, lending him freedom to arrange them
in such a way that the "mystery" of affirmation may
emerge from within the comic convention. And like Shaw,
Fry builds up not only his plots and scenes, but his characters as contrasts and contests of attitudes toward life in
which neither side is necessarily either right or wrong. At
his least successful, in *The Dark is Light Enough* and
some of his religious plays, the supernatural intervenes so
decisively that all ironies and with them the mystery are
obliterated. What sometimes remains is brilliant but

empty verse, unnaturally virtuous characters, and a tangle of incredible motivation.

At his best, however, in *A Phoenix too Frequent, The Lady's not for Burning* and—to a lesser extent—*A Sleep of Prisoners,* Fry integrates the disparate worlds of illusion and reality, traps his characters in a course of events which ironically enhances their stature, and exploits conflicts within the minds of his protagonists between intention and fulfillment, wish and being, and their ideal concepts of themselves and their reality. For instance, in *A Phoenix* Dynamene invokes in richly associative language the image of a husband who was essentially dull and common-place, while the triviality of her motives for seeking death contrasts ironically with her romantic idealism. For his part Tegeus-Chromis is both queasy incompetent and mythic quester. The grotesque pointlessness of his task of guarding corpses makes his yearning for Dynamene's vital-ity and freshness the more appealing, as his imaginative and passionate response to her beauty makes his shortcom-ings all the more farcical. Even Virilius has his part to play. A cadaver with so much power over the living sug-gests the ominous menace of truly malevolent forces, but his shockingly ignominious fate paradoxically implies the existence of equally amazing powers of vitality in the universe.

Thomas Mendip in *The Lady* plays a series of roles which not only express a highly complex personality, but enhance the ultimate mystery which he both affirms in his speech and denies in his person. Court jester, devil's advo-cate, knight in shining armor, deserted soldier, sacrificial victim, displaced aristocrat, and father-protector are only a few of the masks he assumes to both represent and remedy his loss of identity. At the same time his ludicrously exaggerated desire for death makes the keen penetration of his mind all the more tragic in its suffering. And his inability to resist falling in love with the woman who represents all the values he so vociferously rejects makes his failure to have himself hanged all the more comic. And finally, Thomas' death wish is so intense as to make him tragic and comic at the same time (it is no accident that "soul" is both the first and last word in the play). His dramatic invocations of death only increase the disorder, panic, and lust which so endanger Jennet—the helpless victim in the devil's—Thomas'—toils. His insistence on the awakened intelligence demands from him the most uncompromising attacks on illusions of beauty and ideality, placing him in the tradition of tragedy. Yet the ludicrousness of thumbscrews to force a confession of innocence from him, his attempts to convince the woman he loves that life is worthless, and his ultimate surrender to marriage after his furious attacks on male vanity and decay are all comic. There is a diminishing of powers in *Venus Observed,* but there too, an intensely divided protagonist undergoes tragic actions within a comic context. The Duke foolishly assembles his past mistresses and asks his son to choose a new "mother." His misguided manipulation of other peoples' emotions nearly results in his own castration, burning, desertion, and ostracism. But along with the comic apple and mirror tricks, the mistaken identities and bedroom farce, is the tragedy of man in a disvalued world, in a society with intelligence but no culture, in a universe with surprisingly beautiful vegetation and cosmic displays but no God. In its themes it is tragic, while its progression is hilariously comic.

As Bentley has suggested, Fry has adopted the characteristic mode of "tragedy transcended," that is to say, the resolution of revenge through forgiveness. In his religious plays Fry approaches a form which just avoids being "comedy with an unhappy ending" through the appearance of a *deus ex machina.* Cutham's apotheosis, Cymen's Pauline vision of Christ's crucifixion and Moses' "defeat" through the Angel of Death's attack on Rameses are unconvincing intrusions. Only the dream vision technique and the ambiguities of fulfillment lift the onus of contrivance from *A Sleep of Prisoners.* At its most effective the *deus* is handled ironically or parodied with the hanging of Virilius, the "resurrection" of the "buried" Skipps, and the mock-angel flights through the flames of the Duke's two servants. It is hard to tell whether the ambiguous *The Dark* is tragedy with a happy ending or comedy with an unhappy ending, so simple, allegorical and godlike has the character of the countess become.

Fry exploits the incongruities which stem from brokenness as well as the continuity of reality. While one character enacts the miraculous, what he says will mock or undercut it. Love and death are juxtaposed, the presence of one paradoxically heightening and aggravating the emotions which lead to the other. Festivity and sacrifice, vitality and decay, sin and redemption all spring from the integration of tragic and comic which Fry calls the "contention of death with life, which is to say evil with good, which is to say desolation with delight" in "Comedy." His characters have to mock both their own seriousness and frivolity.

Fry is not a philosopher, nor is his thought entirely consistent. But the themes which recur throughout his plays reveal a blend of Christian pacifism, Bergsonian determinism, and humane British liberalism. Like most of his contemporaries he reflects a profound awareness of a fragmented present when the collapse of national states, religious traditions, and class structures has left man adrift in an apparently indifferent universe. "If I try to find my way," Jennet laments in *The Lady*, "I bark my brain / On shadows sharp as rocks where half a day / Ago was a wild soft world." Although Fry has emphatically rejected the pessimism and despair of existentialists like Sartre, Kierkegaard, and others, he is concerned like them with the meaning of identity in the modern world, the nature of good and evil, the possibility of fulfillment in contemporary society and the possibility and meaning of action in an ethical vacuum. Man has found himself torn within and alienated without. The Duke of Altair complains of

> *all tossing and turning*
> *All foundering, all not finding,*
> *All irreconcilability,*
> *All the friction of this great orphanage*
> *Where no one knows his origin and no one*
> *Comes to claim him.*

He is certain only of his desire to live and love when his own consciousness seems to reject any enduring embodiments of these values in this life. David rejects the "victory" Adams claims to have brought back in *A Sleep of Prisoners*: "So many times you've come back . . . / With something else." Because man is conscious, he is separated from nature. He realizes that he alone of living beings experiences the natural evil which is death and the social evil which is war.

> *So any lion can BE, and any ass,*
> *Any any cockatoo. . . .*
> *While I go pestering and wandering down hill*
> *Like a half-wit angel strapped to the back of a mule.*

Man alone experiences panic and emptiness, lacking the comfortable in-itselfness of being which rocks, plants, and animals possess.

Although topical comment is rare in Fry, his search for a norm, for an established social standard of morality expresses his reaction to unremitting change and its resulting disorientations. Yet this flux is nothing new historically, he believes. Only *Venus Observed* has a contemporary setting. Fry's preference for history plays—set in tenth-century England, classical Ephesus, biblical Egypt, and others—implies his sense of unchanging human nature. Most people in all periods of history, Fry implies, are the victims of circumstances and their own emotions. Only a chosen few manage to penetrate life's "miracles and mysteries." Fry seems to distrust radical and political ideologies which promise progress through violence and social reorganization. "Give me civilization, Miss Fleming," Reedbeck comments in *Venus*. "You can keep / Your progress."

Sin and evil are component parts of human nature in his plays, despite the efforts of some of Fry's critics to stress his belief in the goodness of all life and all people. In *Thor, with Angels*, for instance, Tadfrid believes "the gods were formed / Out of the old hurt pride of rejected chaos / which is still lusting for the body of the world we walk on" and the despairing Anath laments in *The First-born,*

> *the muck*
> *Which the sweet gods thought fit to make us of*
> *When they first formed man, the primal putrescence*
> *We keep hidden under our thin dress of health.*

Thomas Mendip insists from the very beginning of *The Lady,* "Here I am, the true phenomenon of acknowledged guilt," and "I / am a figure of vice and crime," "guilty of mankind. I have perpetrated human nature." The inebriated ragpicker Skipps parodies the liturgy: "And immersion upon us miserable offenders. Miserable offenders all—no offence meant." And the Duke claims, "My original / Syntax, like original sin, grows vastier / In the dark."

The sins at the root of human nature stem not from a viciously organized economic system as in Brecht, or the love-hate disparity at the basis of sexual relationships as in Strindberg and O'Neill, or the rigidity and deathlike sterility which overtake all human systems in Shaw. Fry's characters are stricken with narcissistic vanity and selfishness. This self-centeredness emerges in all kinds of symptomatic fixations—personal, social and cosmic—which warp and distort human personality. Faced with chaos, instability, and guilt, many characters regress to comforting images of childhood pleasure and security, withdraw to proud isolation, or threaten suicide. The theme of primitivism is never far from the crux of Fry's plays, as characters often recall or imagine themselves as children. The rebirth of love in Dynamene's heart reminds Tegeus of an early encounter with her when "A star / Ran through me, to live in the brooks of my blood forever." Alizon and Richard exchange childhood reminiscences in *The Lady,* as do Jennet and Thomas. All Fry's characters lament the maturity which brought death to their childlike innocence.

> *O heavens, we have all been young,*
> *Young all day long, young in and out of season,*

In the dream, in the glass, in the firelight—
Perfectly young, obstreperously golden.
What a martyrdom it was.

This is why a sudden, unlooked-for passion is described as "the babe born in the fire," the cupid which emerges from the phoenix's pyre. Rameses associates Moses with a long-forgotten uncle "who is somehow in my memory." Even the Duke believes that "Age, after all, is only the accumulation / Of extensive childhood," and David, in *A Sleep of Prisoners*, plays a series of dependent, childlike roles to escape the impact of cruel, purposeless violence.

Dreams are another refuge from reality, but a less secure one. They threaten to dissolve into visions of terror as the characters quest backwards and within. *A Sleep* resembles a Joycean world with no clear boundary between sleep and wakefulness, although the conflict between truth and illusion is sharper in Fry's more naturalistic *Curtmantle*. Merlin's dream of "the singular shape of the dream dissolving," for example, is a romantic version of the expressionistic nightmare sequence in *Curtmantle*. The roaring holocaust in *Venus Observed*, the sweeping approach of the Angel of Death in *The Firstborn*, and the hanging of Dynamene's dead husband in *A Phoenix* take on a bizarre and farcical tone belying the wish-fulfillment dreams of the protagonists.

Finally, there are the overt and concealed suicide attempts, a motif which Fry had observed in a hospital for shell-shocked patients after the war while he was considering the problem of acting Hamlet. Although he had the reluctant prince in mind, his comments apply to most of his displaced, wandering seekers for identity, from Tegeus-Chromis in *A Phoenix* to Richard Gettner in *The Dark*.

It is the acceptance of his utter separation from all other life in the world: he is outlawed by his own nerves: there *is* no real way of expression for him, except for his heart to break and destroy him: the only possible expression of what he feels, is his own death. . . .[9]

When Tegeus threatens suicide at the end of *A Phoenix*, he wishes to avoid a worse punishment for negligence. Thomas Mendip, however, is modeled on a convict who confessed falsely to a murder, "seeing that life was not really worth living," and the guilt-ridden Rosabel in *Venus* pleads, after her arson has been discovered, "I want harshness. I want hatred." Finally, Gettner openly embraces a form of suicide, atoning for Janik as the Countess had atoned for him.

But if Life is the supreme good, the supreme evil is to destroy it. Life consists of love for Life. It is not merely a limited passion for some other human being. It is a general affection for all that lives, man and animal. This is why Fry's martyrs, the helpless, atoning figures are afraid to die. They are martyrs in spite of themselves, for they know that self-destruction is not a heroic act but foolishness or criminality. On the other hand, aside from Gettner whose death is ambiguous, the desire for martyrdom by those who actively seek their doom is attacked, laughed at, or soothed away by forgiveness and pity. Man learns to resist evil by goodness. His responsibility lies not in imposing his moral standards on life, but in accepting life, however wryly, as his body crumbles into dust.

Another aspect of human communion needs consideration, however. Only two of Fry's plays, his first two comedies, end with marriage and then not with unalloyed bliss. Only a quick wit and lively apprehension snatch Tegeus and Dynamene from a yawning grave. The last-minute rescue of Thomas and Jennet is no less precipitous, but their passion is tempered by a deeper insight into love's pitfalls. "I love you," Thomas admits, "but the world's not changed." At its purest and most innocent, love-at-first-sight strikes characters caught in the situation of Romeo and Juliet, of children baffled by an adult situation. But after *A Phoenix*, they are all minor characters: Richard and Alizon in *The Lady*, Hoel and Martina in *Thor*, Rameses and Phipa (it is suggested) in *The First-born*, and—at their first meeting—Henry II and Eleanor in *Curtmantle* loved blindly, passionately, and sentimentally. They are true, but unconscious, vessels of the Life Force.

Though marriage is the culmination of love at its best, Fry has yet to portray a happily-married couple in his plays. If the desire to idealize one another is humans' greatest urge, alienation is their deepest fear. Yet marriage, ironically, forms the shoals of soul communion. From Virilius in *A Phoenix* to Seti in *The Firstborn*, Humphrey in *The Lady*, the brothers in *Thor*, Dominic in *Venus*, and Henry in *Curtmantle*, Fry's characters often treat vital, intangible human love as a commodity which is static, undemanding, and essentially dead. Marriage replaces genuine love with possessiveness, adoration with buying and selling. His bargainers in affection are the other, cynical side of the coin from his passionate egoists. Yet if husband and wife do appear, the wife is either a shrew as in *Thor* and *Venus* or suppliant as in *The Dark*, or a combination of the two. Fry usually balances his escapist, dishonored, soldiering males with deserted, forlorn females who are often widowed, insulted, or otherwise oppressed. Cuthman's mother and Mrs. Fipps in *The Boy* and Miriam and Anath in *The Firstborn* are only a few examples. Fry seems to suggest that the "twin-hearted permanence" which the Duke in *Venus* idealizes is a distant hope, if not an illusion. It exists only in a remote future, or perhaps in another mode of being like the love-death joining of Gettner and the Countess in *The Dark*. Since love ideally is Life, it can spring only from the shifting, spontaneous relations between man and man, parent and child, ruler and citizen, although unremitting change may have destroyed traditional sanctions for these ties forever.

Finally, Fry brings to grief a series of obsessed, utopian, empire builders whom he views with ambiguous admiration and censure. Virilius in *A Phoenix* is a stodgy and unimaginative bureaucrat who fully deserves his fate. Beginning with *The Firstborn*, however, Fry's system-bound imposters see themselves as embodiments of the historical *élan* who see the state as an ego-fulfiller. Although Seti is

humiliated and broken at the end, his view of the state has
its flashes of grandeur.

> *Nature is lavish*
> *And in return for being understood*
> *Not hoarded, gives us civilization.*
> *Would you have the earth never see purple*
> *Because the murex dies?*

The brothers in *Thor* and David in *A Sleep* never develop
beyond confused, desperate stock types, but Henry in
Curtmantle exhausts the love of friends, wife, and family
in his tireless quest for the perfect state. He dies stripped
and defeated, though not without having aspired with the
pride of Tamburlaine and the ambition of Faust. Because
a vision of perfection is so fluid, fortuitous, and spontaneous, it may overwhelm the idealist. Its mystery may
unbalance his sense of values. As a result the flux of
energies within the universe may be constricted into the
sterile, self-defeating war of good and evil which leaves no
middle ground, no room for growth and accommodation.

At base it is not nature or society which is chaotic but
human nature, which embodies the ancient split between
reason and emotion, finite and infinite, God and man.
"When the thoughts are alert for life, the instincts rage
for destruction," says Dynamene in *A Phoenix* and
Thomas extends the image in *The Lady*.

> *We have given you a world as contradictory*
> *As a female, as cabbalistic as the male,*
> *A conscienceless hermaphrodite who plays*
> *Heaven off against hell, hell off against heaven,*
> *Revolving in the ballroom of the skies*
> *Glittering with conflict as with diamonds.*

The Duke discovers that "everyone's heart is a great eccentric" and Perpetua that "what is *my* freedom
becomes / Another person's compulsion. What are we to
make / Of this dilemma?" And Hoel in *Thor* is amazed.
"What simple-witted things the affections are, / That
can't perceive whether people are enemies / Or friends."

Although conflicts pitting individuals against other individuals, against groups, ideas, and situations occur in Fry, they do not determine the outcome. What happens instead is that the protagonist stubbornly resists a blessing. The relation of divine and mundane, God and man, as Nelvin Vos points out, is not man's painful, often fruitless pursuit of God as in Eliot, but that of man's eyes being opened to his sinful selfishness which is obscuring the persistent and ever-present workings of gracious love around and within him.[10] Instead of the character only wishing to do or acquire something and in the process meeting opposition, in Fry's best plays the protagonists must also, in Mandel's words, "succumb to a blessing." They are subdued by good, by the power of love. Therefore the usual action is a depiction of sacrificial love of one individual who atones for the other. Fry's belief in the proper balance of opposites, reason and instinct, appearance and reality appears not only in motivation and action, but in his cosmos. For accompanying the ritual movement of life and death, atonement and resurrection is the creative evolution of things from unperceived germ to the shape and nature latent in them.

At his best Fry creates a romantic atmosphere in which the possibility of happiness and love arises—but whether as illusion or reality remains uncertain, as in *A Phoenix* and *The Lady*. Love dissolves in the cosmic mystery of illusion and reality. Thus the concept of mystery is central to his technique. The term "mystery" suggests two aspects. First, it has the ordinary sense of the unexplained, the mystifying, the uncanny. Fry has in mind the irrationality of life, of human motives, particularly in such matters as pacifism. In *A Sleep* Peter asks, "How can I help it if I can't work myself up / About the way things go? It's a mystery to me." Moses in *The Firstborn* speaks of "the mystery of existing / At all" and later asks, "Shall we live in mystery and yet / Conduct ourselves as though everything were known?" Fry speaks in his essay on *The Lady* of "a world which has deeps and shadows of mystery." This kind of mystery evades the modern passion for labeling, for pigeonholding, resulting in the wonder of the accidental, the hitherto unperceived, a fresh perspective. As Thomas Mendip puts it to the rationalist Jennet, "We have wasted paradox and mystery on you / When all you ask us for is cause and effect!" All these pulsing, glittering, clashing elements have a danger, however:

> The vision of an anxious man is likely to dwindle; his anxiety becomes his world, and his world of anxiety may become despair. Or, at least, he may be so immersed in the immediate struggle that he becomes lost to the larger struggle of which this is a moment.[11]

The "larger struggle" suggests a second, complementary aspect of mystery. This is the Chaplain's "eternity in the passing moment," the platonic oneness which unifies diversity. The medieval sense of microcosm within and reflecting the macrocosm has long since been shattered, but Fry hopes at least provisionally to restore man's link with God, the world with the cosmos.

> It is better that we should simplify towards a unity than towards a shoddy system of labels; towards an admission that everything and everyone is a member one of another, a unity of difference, where all things meet in gradation, offsetting each other, dovetailing, completing, complementing, rather than towards the official chaos where nothing entirely belongs to the drawer it was put into.[12]

The progression of the action toward this mystic unity involves more than the discovery of the culprit in a "whodunit": rather it proceeds dialectically. Characters who embody impartial, incomplete ideas of mystery are often pitted against one another. One holds a utopian, but authoritarian view of an ideal society which he as self-ordained symbol of his peoples' aspirations struggles to embody. The other, the stronger one, contends against these with ideas less palatable to human egotism, less intolerant, less acceptable in terms of human pride. This struggle contributes to the "laddering of effects toward an over-all tonal roof" that Arrowsmith has perceived in Fry's drama, aimed at revealing finally that the commonplace, when properly seen, is miraculous. Fry says,

I am using the word mystery in the sense of a what-am-I? In Chapter One we are presented with a life; then with a succession of clues, intimations of a truth which is so profound that we can't reach it by rational deduction; and if we listen to those intimations—to what, indeed, is revealed of God—we end with a greater life than we began with.[13]

As Vos has pointed out, mystery to Fry is both something hidden and something revealed, for revelation itself inevitably partakes of mystery. And here lies the fundamental meaning of mystery for Fry: what man really does in his living in mystery is to search out the ways of God. Both aspects of mystery are found in man and in his world because they are found in the nature of Godhead.

The frequently advanced critical view that Fry contrasts a concept of a mysterious poetic universe with that of a dull, routine reality without depth or joy is mistaken. Fry has certainly referred to wonder and mystery, to the state of cosmic surprise in which many of his characters dwell. "Life has such / Diversity. I sometimes lose / Eternity in the passing moment," as the Chaplain in *The Lady* says. But the sense that all events take place as though by miracle is, as Mandel points out, not the issue, but the climate of the plays. Fry does not pit "marvellers against nonmarvellers" as some of his detractors have suggested, or the perceptive against the unperceptive as Eliot does. Many of Fry's characters who are untouched by a consciousness of mystery still are capable of affection and love. Fry's protagonists differ from them only by their intelligence of Life. Hostile critics such as Donoghue have pointed to a phrase such as "what we *call* reality is a false god, the dull eye of custom" as indicative of his equation of "Prose with Verisimilitude," and of "Poetry with Truth." Donoghue has conveniently ignored Fry's irony, the balance of disparates in both his theory and practice, for Fry believes,

> Prose and verse existing side by side counter each other's dangers. If they pass altogether out of each other's reach they cease to be themselves, becoming on the one hand

journalese, official cant, or any other string of sentences: and on the other, a vagueness, an abstraction, a preciousness. This interplay of difference, one touching the hand of the other as it separates, like men and women dancing the Great Chain, is what keeps each in its own state of grace.[14]

Fry rejects simple antitheses: appearance, reality; actual, real; fact, miracle; prose, poetry. As he says,

> The outward face of the world has infinite variety; action of any kind, from the trivial to the heroic, can absorb our days and leave us gasping for time. . . . All would be wed with my life of prose if there were not moments . . . when the extreme diversity of life threatens to disintegrate altogether unless it can be unified in some place of the mind.[15]

Like Swift, Wilde, and Shaw, the invisible ironists, Fry is a character in his own plays. He visualizes an audience that sympathetically shares in the moment of the plays toward the creation of an idealized Fry-persona. In the character of the Duke of Altair in Venus, for example, "Talent, conversation, wit, / Ease and friendliness are all swallowed up / In advance." But his understanding is cultivated more than his reason, his urbane sensitivity more than his moral straitness. His detractors, like Rosabel, fail to see this. Elsewhere Fry says of his persona:

> He needs all his senses and perceptions to keep him aware of what his existence represents. He needs every property of mind he possesses, all those attributes which most curiously distinguish him from his fellow animals—compassion, laughter, concern beyond his own immediate neighborhood, a sense of mystery, of his own incompleteness, and much more. He needs to think and feel in detail as deeply as he thinks and feels in general. . . . The ultimate answer to most of our problems is in the growth towards maturity of each individual.[16]

He is a cultivated, educated gentleman with a gently ironic detachment. To taste and sophistication he adds a rich fancy. His original mind is genuinely inspired by a liberal, humane sympathy and he has a perceptive and acute rather than a deeply speculative mind.

2

The Boy with a Cart

The Boy with a Cart [1] is Fry's first published play, the only one to appear in print before the war, in 1939. It was written in 1937 at the request of the vicar in the Sussex village of Colman's Hatch to commemorate the fiftieth anniversary of the church at Steyning. In both the legend and Fry's treatment which closely follows it, Cuthman leaves his home on a pilgrim's progress with his mother. He finally arrives in Steyning where he has been inspired to build a church, after overcoming a series of obstacles which Fry has called "sorrows." (The term may come from Isaiah 53:3: "a man of sorrows and acquainted with grief.")

Three years after *Murder in the Cathedral* was presented at the Canterbury Festival in 1935, Fry adopted the same three-level scheme of character presentation used in *Murder,* as Eliot has described it in his introduction to Pascal's *Pensées*: the chorus is placed in the order of nature; the villagers, Cuthman's various antagonists and his mother in the order of the mind; and Cuthman in the order of charity, along with the chorus. While the miracles which happen in the play seem incredible or comic to the earth-bound types, their "true" significance is revealed through Cuthman's church-building mission. Appropriately Fry's choral "People of South England" speak image-clogged, irregularly-rhymed verse like Eliot's Women of Canterbury; like Eliot's murderers, minor characters speak racier prose. Cuthman uses both. The themes of martyrdom and church-building as in Eliot's *The Rock* are utilized, and the sun-image becomes Fry's equivalent for the wheel Louis Martz has singled out as Eliot's presiding image.

Cuthman is an enthusiastic adolescent whose sheep-herding has Davidic overtones, to say nothing of the magic circle he has drawn to keep his herd from wandering. Stanford has found evidence of Fry's fondness for his father in Cuthman's speeches about his dead father.

> Each morning my father buckles himself to,
> Like a leather strap, and at night comes to the fire
> His hands bare with well-water to tell
> The story of Jesus.

Yet there is resentment, and even guilt too, in Cuthman's plea.

> What have I done? Did I steal God away
> From my father to guard my sheep . . .
> What sin brought in the strain, the ominous knock,
> The gaping seam? . . . What have I done to him?

The implied oedipal motif becomes overt in many of the later plays such as *Thor, Venus, A Sleep,* and *Curtmantle,* where sons attack or even try to kill their fathers.

Cuthman is forced to cope in rapid succession with the shocking news that his father is dead and that he is dispossessed. Building a cart, he sets off across South England with his mother, a fine comic foil. She is commonsensical, grumpy, talkative, a fatalist who enlivens his progress with pungent complaints. "Sometimes I think you can't be very well, Cuthman." Empson would call her a fool in a wise situation.

In the next scene Cuthman meets a group of mocking harvesters who ridicule the fall of Cuthman's mother from the cart when the cart rope breaks. Their song is lively, inspired doggerel which they sing as Cuthman and his mother go off to make a new rope of willow twigs.

> Don't fall into the stream, Mother.
> The water's very high.
> We might not hear you scream, Mother.
> And we'd hate to see you die!

But as the satyrlike mowers go back to their fields, a
destructive rainstorm ruins their crops, bringing Cuthman a new epiphany (resembling Christ's vision after his
baptism by John). He has learned that he must go as far
as the withies hold, and on the spot where they break:
"The church / And I shall be built together; and
together / Find our significance."

The rope breaks at Steyning. The villagers welcome
them, giving them a home and work. Fry has enough plot
here for several plays, but old Tawm, who is to marry
Cuthman's mother, is a fine touch, with his crotchety wit
and his refusal to be coddled. Cuthman's idea for erecting
a church is supported by the townspeople with gusto.
Only the recalcitrant Fipps brothers oppose the church-
building project. After six months, disgusted by their failure even to "put up a shove-ha'penny team against Bram-
ber" (a mile away), they slyly pen up Cuthman's oxen.
The angry young man yokes and drives them in place of
the oxen, while their protesting, fiery mother is carried
away by a divine whirlwind, "zipzag like a paper bag, like
somebody's hat!" and mock-baptized in a bog.

In the last scene, two years later, Cuthman finally
achieves spiritual maturity. Previously characterized
successively as sorcerer's apprentice, poet, warrior, and
priest, he becomes vicarious martyr. The king post has
slipped in the nearly completed church, and the workers
cannot put it back. For the moment despair overcomes
them, even Cuthman, who "has gone into a ghost." But
he runs in to report that a figure has appeared to him.

> He stretched his hand upon it, at his touch
> It lifted to its place. There was no sound.
> I cried out, and I cried at last "Who are you?"
> I heard him say "I was a carpenter". . . .

As before, the exciting and miraculous actions occur offstage, to be reported by a messenger or the chorus after the
fact.

The action which all the characters share—through in-
spiration, persuasions, or duress—is "to build a church," to

form through this action "a perspective to the vision." The agonizing tension and inner conflict in the mind of Eliot's Becket have given way to a zesty, spontaneous faith. Just as the cart is a literal and dramatic "vehicle" for Cuthman's mother, so is Cuthman a vehicle for God's will. Then too, Cuthman gains stature not through struggle, but from the height to which he is miraculously raised. But because the miracles which appear in the play are so compelling, they coerce the action. Because they are so obvious, they fail to induce a sense of mystery, except as a stock response.

Yet the plot's simplicity is partly deceptive. Complicating Cuthman's single-minded search are journeys at cross-purposes: back and forth (from village to village, desert to meadow, farm to town), and up and down (stairs, hills and valleys, sky and earth). At the same time the homely, realistic pragmatism of Cuthman's mother is balanced by the lofty idealism of the chorus. When at first the cart and then the church are built, future becomes past and Son finally redeems saint, Fry clearly intends that the audience be lifted out of time and space on to the plane of the universal, with an echo from Eliot's *The Rock*.

> *What of us who have to catch up, always*
> *To catch up with the high-powered car, or with*
> *The unbalanced budget, to cope with competition,*
> *To weather the sudden thunder of the uneasy*
> *Frontier . . . Between*
> *Our birth and death we may touch understanding*
> *As a moth brushes a window with its wing.*

One can see at a glance the derivative nature of the play. The time-setting somewhere between the early Middle Ages and the present, the liturgical mode and particularly the choral idiom can be tracked through Eliot's snow, a debt Fry has many times acknowledged.

Fry's choral speeches often replace metaphors with repetitive phrases and abstractions in Eliot's manner.

> *Out of this, out of the first incision*
> *Of mortality on mortality, there comes*

> *The genuflexion, and the partition of pain*
> *Between man and God; there grows the mutual action,*
> *The perspective to the vision.*

As in Eliot, most of the chorus' ideas and images are lost on even the most attentive audience. In finding his own idiom, Fry was to turn to sources as diverse as the German poet Rainer Maria Rilke, the nineteenth-century dramatist T. L. Beddoes, and his older contemporary Charles Williams. We can compare lines from Fry's chorus:

> *In our fields, fallow and burdened, in grass and furrow*
> *In barn and stable, with scythe, flail, or harrow,*
> *Sheepshearing, milking or mowing, on labour that's older*
> *Than knowledge, with God we work shoulder to shoulder;*
> *God providing, we dividing, sowing, and pruning;*
> *Not knowing yet and yet sometimes discerning . . .*

with Charles Williams' lines from his play *Seed of Adam*: [2]

> *Dullards of darkness, light's lazybones,*
> *poor primitives of our natural bareness,*
> *where's your awareness? Will moans and groans*
> *for gold or brawn or brain regain*
> *the way to the entry of Paradise? up!*

Yet Fry's verse is notably easier for the actor to speak than Williams' idiosyncratic alliteration and internal rhymes, his choppy rhythms.

Despite echoes from his older contemporaries, Fry's verse is appropriately varied. In the choral speech which describes the journey Cuthman and his mother take, most of the merits of his style are evident.

> *Stone over stone, over the shaking track,*
> *They start their journey: jarring muscle and aching*
> *Back crunch the fading county into*
> *Dust. Stone over stone, over the trundling*
> *Mile, they stumble and trudge: where the thirsty bramble*
> *Begs at the sleeve, the pot-hole tugs the foot.*

The long vowels of "stone over stone" become a labored refrain, and "shaking track" chimes mockingly against "aching back." Fry's replacement of concrete with abstract nouns ("county" for "road") and his pathetic fallacy ("trundling mile") all indicate his metaphysical tendencies. Fry's expository speeches are hypermetric, but action is usually expressed in regular blank verse. And in both the prose and verse sections, anapests indicate travel: "You needn't go farther than the end of the earth to find a fortune."

The Boy has achieved an afterlife in the limbo of religious theater, but it is less important in itself than in its promise for the future. Fry would never again echo quite so studiously the verse of T. S. Eliot, Charles Williams or W. H. Auden, to name only a few. Nor would he construct again an action so episodic, so clearly modeled on Bunyan's *Pilgrim's Progress*. But harbingers for the postwar plays lie in his modulation of a tragic action into a comic outcome, the scenic contrast of wasteland with edenic garden, a focus on the culture hero and his vision of a theocratic state, the witty and exuberant rhetoric, and the literal or parodied intervention of the *deus ex machina*. These archetypal patterns and devices are to form much of his intuitive grasp of the theatrical form from which Fry will shape his ensuing dramatic works.

3

The Firstborn

The Firstborn [1] has had a checkered career both in print and in the theater. Fry began work on it in 1938, finishing the first version in 1945. It was published in 1946, broadcast by the B.B.C. in 1947 and first performed legitimately at the Edinburgh Festival, where it opened in September, 1948. The second version was presented in London in January of 1952; the third was produced in New York in April, 1958, where it played for a limited six-week engagement with Katharine Cornell and Anthony Quayle in the lead roles. Between the first and second versions, Fry made extensive "alterations and cuts" which squeezed the fat out of many of the verbose speeches and toned down Moses' self-inflation, such as "I could be Pharaoh in Midian." [2] Fry also dropped a long scene in which Teusret, the Pharaoh's daughter speaks rather cynically of her father's opportunism, casting a cloud over her otherwise untainted simplicity. Fry made a few more cuts and changes between the second and third versions of the play, but he was mainly concerned with stressing Moses' impact on Rameses, the Pharaoh's doomed firstborn, a fleeting motivation which escaped most of his auditors. Since writing the play Fry has commented wryly he has been learning "too reluctantly that neither audiences nor critics are clairvoyant." [3]

Fry owes the bare outline of his plot to the first twelve chapters of Exodus which recount the miraculous freeing of Moses from the Nile and his preservation by the Pharaoh's daughter, only to be exiled and later return to free the Israelites from another Pharaoh's oppression. From the fabulous encounter of a semi-divine culture hero and a woodenly obstinate trickster, Fry has selected a few climactic days. And within an enclosed, claustrophobic setting, the action moves toward its ironic conclusion: the birth of Israel's freedom from the death of Egypt's best hope. Fry has reduced Moses' forty years of exile in Midian to a decade which goes along with the change in Moses from the tongue-tied octogenarian of the Bible to a passionate spellbinder of around fifty. "The character of Moses," Fry says in the "Foreword," "is a movement toward maturity, toward a balancing of life within the mystery, where the conflicts and dilemmas are the trembling of the balance" (vii). Although he is conceived on a vaster, more ambitious scale, Moses' germ had appeared dimly at the end of *The Boy*. He is the Carlylean "great man," building a new spiritual community on the ruins of an old one. However, the greater focusing of the scene, alternating between the Pharaoh's palace and Miriam's tent, and the sophistication of the antagonists presage *A Phoenix too Frequent* and the comedies. And despite the play's ostensible setting in 1200 B.C., the talk of pogroms, slave labor and genocide has an ominously modern echo from the concentration camps and mass murder of World War II.

The returning Moses is seen, first of all, through the eyes of the Egyptian royal family, each of them having a limited function in mind for him. To the Pharaoh's sister, son, and daughter, he is something of a mystery, a legendary figure half-composed of dreams. "I thought he was a dust-storm we had shut outside." Tormented by the screams of dying Hebrew slaves and the thunder of rumbling stone from which a pyramid is being built, the Pharaoh's sister Anath and her niece Teusret tell their tales while the Pharaoh, an imagined Seti II, impatiently awaits the onetime felon and general: "I need Moses—we have discarded in him / A general of excellent perception." Seti faces mounting problems of invasion from without and dissension within his realm and needs Moses to lead his troops.

When Moses enters for a prodigal's triumph, all sins forgiven, he brushes aside the proffered welcome. Rejecting the Egyptian mantle of borrowed greatness, he adopts the alienated, dishonored role of Israelite outsider. Moses has been reborn from adversity: "The prince of Egypt died. I am the Hebrew / Smitten out of the shadow of that prince." He at first speaks riddlingly of his weeping blood from Egypt, but when Seti presses him to again accept an Egyptian commission, the two men begin quarreling, struggling with less and less success to maintain their urbane, calmly purposeful sophistication. Moses rejects Seti's conciliatory attempts, standing aside to let his brother Aaron jab away at Seti's crimes against the captive Israelite nation. Aaron is a methodical, totally dedicated plain dealer whose understated statistical manner at last shakes Seti's tenacious air of calm. Once Aaron accuses the Pharaoh directly, this makes him attack in return, and the primary opponents begin to trade blow for blow. "This is intolerable / Singsong! Am I to compose the epitaphs / For every individual grave of this trying summer?" Face to face, the fighters each try to bend the other to his will while each is forced, in contrast to the limited, fragmentary goals of all the other characters, to see his motives in the broadest possible perspective. Enslaving, torturing, and killing the Israelites for the sake of his deathly pyramid, Seti believes he has "put men to a purpose who otherwise / Would have had not the least meaning." Moses, for his part, champions a fully contemporary, humane individualism, an idea which is expressed throughout Fry's plays.

> It is the individual man
> In his individual freedom who can mature
> With his warm spirit the unripe world.

Balked by Moses' obstinacy, Seti withdraws in barely concealed anger, his purpose shaken and his policy momentarily frustrated.

The conventional clash of stiff-necked visionary with his equally stubborn persecutor is a dramatic projection of the pattern Hegel perceived behind the greatest tragedies, notably Sophocles' *Antigone*. It is not so much the war of good with evil which embodies the essential tragic conflict, but the war of good with good, abstractly conceived: "We're not enemies so much / As creatures of division," Moses tells Rameses. When two of these "powers" are in conflict, making incompatible demands, they not only pit representatives of two warring societies against one another, but split each of the groups with internal dissension and divide their leaders against themselves. On the one hand, the Pharaoh is torn within, between his desire for political survival and his need for family affection and loyalty. On the other, as Seti drifts farther and farther into blind intransigiency, Moses' conflict with God becomes the focal point of the play's interest.

The second scene is another maimed ceremony of homecoming, shifting from the open, sunlit terrace of Egyptian rationalism to the closed, stifling tent of Moses' sister Miriam. Her despair ironically widens the spiritual scene beyond the constricted vistas of her airless tent. In the distance, outside the "withering city," lie the parched mountains and beyond them, the watchful powers of retribution. Like Eliot's Women of Canterbury, Miriam finds "little difference / Between ourselves and those blindfolded oxen. / We also do the thing we cannot see." As Moses gropes for a way to help good "be strong enough to break out of the possessing / Arms of evil," Rameses arrives. He urges Moses to guarantee Egypt's safety by becoming her general, directing in this way Seti's goodwill toward the Israelites. Rejected by Moses as immature and unrealistic, Rameses makes one last appeal for a sense of purpose only Moses can provide. "You / Are clear and risen roundly over the hazes. / You have the formula, I need it."

His outer firmness concealing an inner agitation, Moses recognizes in the boy his own guilt-blighted but once innocent youth. Fry has explained in the "Foreword":

Rameses is the innocence, vigour and worth which stand on the enemy side, not altering the justice or necessity of

Moses' cause, but linking the ways of men and the ways of
God with a deep and urgent question-mark.

After saving Miriam's son Shendi from a beating—the
Hebrew brickmakers have struck—Rameses leaves, humiliated. Moses then confronts a double irony: while the
Egyptians whom Moses has repudiated see him as their
deliverer, the Hebrews he had hoped to lead out of captivity reject him as an unwanted alien. Although he rejects
"thankless palace manoeuvring and compromise," the success of his aims would destroy both Egypt and the prince
he refuses to manipulate. In the largest sense Moses stands
for the inquiry into the strength of good.

> Somewhere, not beyond our scope, is a power
> Participating but unharnessed, waiting
> To be led towards us. Good has a singular strength
> Not known to evil.

But Moses is fated to discover, through his own passionate
desire to make of good a personal instrument, that if
unharnessed good has strength, harnessed good is mixed
with evil, the inevitable failures of its invoker's mind and
will.

In the next scene Rameses learns of his arranged marriage to Phipa of Syria, whose beauty has inspired a rich
lore of folktales. "A figure of her, hung under the
stern / And kissing the wake, ensures a harvest of fish."
While Rameses urges Seti to commission Shendi as a
means of corrupting Moses, Teusret marks her brother's
coming of age with a naïve maturity ritual. But Moses
interrupts her song to accuse Seti again, this time with the
corpse of a crucified Israelite boy. His laconic, bitter attack
echoes the "Stetson" speech in Eliot's *The Waste Land*.

> This is your property.
> Of little value. Shall I bury it in your garden?
> You need have no anxiety. It will not grow.

Once again Moses and Seti stand toe to toe in a cruelly *ad
hominem* debate. Seti mocks Moses' zeal with a vision
which appropriates the prophet's mysticism and olympian
loftiness to himself.

> *Nature is lavish,*
> *And in return for being understood,*
> *Not hoarded, gives us civilization.*
> *Would you have the earth never see purple*
> *Because the murex dies? Blame, dear Moses,*
> *The gods for their creative plan which is*
> *Not to count the cost but enormously*
> *To bring about.*

Yet under the hammer blows of Moses' appeals for individual freedom and his threats to an already tottering regime, Seti's calm disintegrates: "I have nursed you long enough. Now dungeons can nurse you." Although Seti prides himself on stoical wisdom and endurance, his faults are the defects of his virtues: beneath his moderation, empire-building, and statesmanship lurk indecision, an egoistic self-adulation, and pride. Moses is also shaken to his depths. He manages, however, to recall Seti to the purpose they both share: the rediscovery of an inner truth and service of God. "I am here by fury and the heart. Is that not a law?"

Moses' demand for the purification of "the misery of my blood" links his own onetime murder of the Egyptian overseer with Seti's oppressive violence in a single, overriding sin. As Philip Wheelwright has shown in *The Burning Fountain*, for primitive societies murder was a diseased act which spills the victim's blood. The contagion is transmitted to the soil where it spreads throughout the land, sterilizing both the soil and its people. Only a ritual exorcism of the victim's spirit can remove the curse from the wasteland. Moses and Seti both fear and hate "the crippling ghost that haunts us," but their confusion about its identity and purification only further divides them. When Moses invokes God's intervention to second his appeal, the sky is beaten into thunder. However, Moses' idiom has the unfortunate effect of anti-climax by reducing God to a meddling bystander: "What says the infinite eavesdropper?"

The alternation between the Egyptian palace and Israelite tent implies two ways of life. On the Egyptian side, embodied by Seti II, is a world of duty, political expediency, and realism. The Hebrew side, as Moses embodies it, reveals a world of mystical transcendence, self-accusatory guilt and spiritual transformation. Seti believes that mankind is innately worthless; only the unremitting coercion of the masses by their more enlightened leaders will produce the civilized values of order, stability, and beauty. It is ironic that both he and Miriam should compare the social order to nature. This analogy, as William Empson points out in *Some Versions of Pastoral*, gives it a dignity which is undeserved and an inevitability which is unwarranted. Moses, on the other hand, appeals to man's innate goodness; he proposes in essence a return to an untainted Eden where the absence of a restraining, centralized authority will permit an untrammeled blossoming of man's virtues. Yet all the characters in the play, Egyptian and Hebrew alike, are attempting in their contradictory ways, "to find their god and so become living men at last."

Just as the first act presents a series of conflicts resulting from faulty perception, the second act involves suffering which purges the diseased land. Back in Miriam's tent, Moses' increased single-mindedness only further confuses his supporters. His sister Mirian, who has already endured too much pain, cannot understand why Moses must make still more trouble. His brother Aaron, a practical revolutionary, is put off by Moses' mysticism. "Is it not possible still to be plain men / Dealing with a plain situation? Must we see / Visions?" And Moses' nephew Shendi, pleased with his rapid advancement in the Egyptian army, assumes Moses is jealous of his petty success (although the third edition of the play reduces their personal conflict). "Only one of the family must rise / And glow in Egypt." Aaron and Miriam have as much difficulty accepting the arrival of the plagues as Seti had in believing Moses' threats. Moses rejects Anath's appeals for moderation. His refusal to scale down his demands for unconditional surrender ironically alienates his own supporters while hardening Seti's resolve. Yet both Moses and Miriam, with Shendi, have high hopes, all of them soon to be dashed.

In the next palace scene the plagues are reported (like

the offstage miracles in *The Boy* and *Thor, with Angels*).
Time enough for seven plagues has elapsed, each plague
following one of Seti's broken promises: "I'll not be pun-
ished by this chain / Of black coincidence." As calculating
and sceptical as ever, Seti denies any personal wrongdoing.
He pins his hopes on Rameses' marriage, refusing Moses
again. Fry handles the biblical comment that God "hard-
ened his heart" as best he can, tempering Seti's character
with just enough reason to avoid making him a melodramatic psychopath. Ironically, Seti needs Moses both as
general to hold together his crumbling empire and scapegoat to shoulder the consequences of his own indecision.
As Kenneth Burke has put it, they must compete "cooper-
atively." After choking off his son's rebelliousness—Shendi
has become an inhuman monster, thanks to his misguided
promotion—Seti hears of yet another military defeat.
Moses returns to invoke divine judgment, only to be attacked in turn by Anath: "What is this divinity / Which
with no more dexterity than a man / Rips up good things
to make a different kind / Of good?" Moses is forced
to recognize both his ignorance and isolation. The sky
then darkens, a natural manifestation of both Seti's
blind rage and Moses' uncomprehending faith. The hand
of God, Moses believes, has left "man alone with his
baffled brain. / Only Seti can set the sun free," (his words
as acrostic of Seti's name).

The second act is designed to cast doubt on the rationalizations of all the characters, blurring the neat links
between man and God, insight and ignorance, freedom
and bondage. Although Moses' repeated invocations of
divine fury seem a trifle pat, the act is partly effective in
restoring a sense of mystery to the Godhead.

The end of the play focuses on Rameses who, as Fry
points out,

> lives a childhood almost identical with Moses' own; he and
> the Hebrew Shendi between them draw the frontiers of
> combat altogether differently from the lines laid down by
> accepted human action. ("Foreword")

At the literal and symbolic eleventh hour, the Hebrews
have just completed the first Passover ritual. The last, most
terrible divine visitation approaches, to coincide with the
arrival of Rameses' new Syrian bride. In the series of
recognitions which end the play, Aaron accepts the mystery of divine deliverance and Shendi attacks Moses for
the Hebrews' restlessness. First Aaron and then Moses
realize that Rameses is doomed: "The boy / Pays for the
father." Behind Moses' life, and the destiny of an entire
people, lies a pattern of revenge, *lex talionis*, tit for tat.

> God is putting me back with the assassins.
> Is that how he sees me? I killed an Egyptian
> And buried him in the sand. Does one deed then
> Become our immortal shape?

Moses rushes out to Rameses' deliverance, cautioning
Shendi as he goes, but his guilt-ridden nephew tears off his
Egyptian uniform, breaking away into the dark and death.

Moses runs to the palace, hoping that he and the royal
family can form a death-defying circle of life around
Rameses. Dramatic pathos is heightened as Rameses'
bride Phipa literally, but hopelessly, races the Angel of
Death to the boy's side. Despite Moses' desperate appeal
for unity against death, Rameses dies. For the Egyptians
his death signals the collapse of a society with nothing to
replace it, leaving despair and grief. In Rameses they have
lost a boy who represents the nobler, more unselfish elements of both Moses and Seti. The survivors have become
united only by their recognition that the necessary destruction of evil carries with it the waste of great good, as
Bradley has observed of Shakespeare. Moses "suffers victory" and leaves, accepting the ultimate unknowability of
God. "I do not know why the necessity of God / Should
feed on grief; but it seems so." Yet he hopes that good will
ultimately extend to all men.

> We must each find our separate meaning
> In the persuasion of our days
> Until we meet in the meaning of the world.
> Until that time.

The conclusion of the play is effective, however, only if Fry has established a clear basis for Moses' concern for the young prince. In retrospect, he has recognized this weakness.

The critics felt, very reasonably, that the affection between Moses and Rameses had been so barely touched on that three-quarters of the impact of Moses' realization was lost.

Now I had not imagined any such personal affection on the part of Moses. In the play he meets Rameses for a bare five minutes; is touched by his hero worship; recognizes the boy's sincerity and humanity, and that is all. What I hoped I had shown, and hadn't, was that to Moses the boy represented Moses' own boyhood when he was Prince of Egypt, represented also that love for Egypt which Moses couldn't shake off even while he was fighting her. There are certainly speeches to that effect, and Moses, in the moment of realization, cries, "Egypt! Egypt! He was meant for Egypt!"; but the speeches were not enough.[4]

The style of the play is obviously early Fry, although he has tried in his revisions to move toward the spareness of A *Sleep of Prisoners* and *Curtmantle*. While the tumbling, exuberant language of the comedies is played off against the witty scepticism of the characters, there are some lapses in *The Firstborn*. Fry has difficulty at times with his omniscient, waiting God, "the infinite eavesdropper," although the Hebrew deity of vengeance is presented forcefully enough.

> It is the God of the Hebrews, a vigour moving
> In a great shadow, who draws the bow
> Of his mystery, to loose this punishing arrow
> Feathered with my fate.

That Fry has often been able to lift several lines out of the middle of a long speech without changing its meaning indicates the verbosity of the verse. He has Teusret speak of "the noise a flute makes / When the mouth's too full of saliva," which is fairly enlightening. When Rameses says, "the future / Has suddenly come up, two legged, huge, as though to say / 'See nothing but me,' " the figure is promising, but in the end it collapses into statement rather than into meaningful surprise. And some of the time the diction is flat: "Get yourself another heir!"

Yet the ornate, elaborate language is often admirably suited for its purpose: "Egypt is only / One golden eruption of time, one flying spark / Attempting the ultimate fire." At times, Fry works in a striking aphorism which sums up the matter perfectly. "Statesmanship," says Seti, "is the gods' gift to restrain their own / Infidelities to man."

Just as the play represents a cosmos of puzzles and mystery, the idiom is substantially interrogative, often distractingly so, with question answering question. The most disturbed and frightened characters—notably Miriam—stutter, break off in the middle of sentences, and speak in fragments, while those with more self-control play with words, as in "outmove motives" or "approaches the unapproachable."

In the course of the action Fry establishes a series of contrasts: palace and tent, garden and desert, role and identity, honesty and guile, nature and God, sickness and health, and others. He has also paired and contrasted his characters, making the advocates of disinterested compromise, Aaron and Seti, foils for the more inspired visionaries Moses and Rameses. Complementing the return of nemesis for a crime of blood, the action pits Hegelian good against good. Seti and Rameses are both torn by double obligations, their family ties on one hand, and their duties as leaders on the other. Rameses is also torn between the appeals of Seti's statesmanship and Moses' mysticism, calculation and vision, father and father-substitute. Ironically, Rameses is forced to accept the throne without power, guilt without responsibility, as a Christlike figure whose death indicts his entire society. Seti, on the other hand, hastens the very crisis he had struggled to forestall, preserving his throne at the cost of the social and political immortality which gave it meaning.

Moses faces a similar but more complex dilemma. He is an Adamic figure who finally assumes full responsibility for the consequences of his "original sin." He chooses, therefore, to live in a purgatory of his own making until he has been purged of sin. He too is torn between familial and social roles, but he is also both hero and scapegoat, aggressor and victim. However, the outcome of his struggle, unlike Seti's, is fully determined in advance. Yet he is only partly enlightened at the beginning, as shortsighted and single-minded in his dedication to Hebrew freedom as Seti had been toward Egyptian supremacy. The end of *The Firstborn* demonstrates not the wrongness of opposing claims, but the denial of the exclusive assertions of one rather than the other.

Fry has chosen to represent both the force behind history against which man's efforts appear ineffectual and puny, and the human aspirations which shape this force into coherent significance. Once again, man's character becomes his fate. For while the men on either side develop the action in time through their internecine conflicts, the women represent the interests of that resolution. For all the play's shortcomings, *The Firstborn* is an ambitious play which deals competently and in an interesting way with most of the themes which will occupy Fry for the rest of his career.

4

A Phoenix too Frequent

When Fry was able to return to the Oxford Playhouse and writing in 1944, he deliberately chose verse as his literary medium. "It seems to have been just the right moment," he told the *New York Times*.

> I lay the acceptance of poetry in the theatre nowadays to two things. One is the reaction to the long hold of "surface realism." The other is that the world seems rather cut down a bit. . . . And poetry provides something people lack and wish for: a richness and a reaffirmation.[1]

For a year Fry became one of two resident dramatists in London's private Arts Theatre Club, finishing the one-act *A Phoenix too Frequent*.[2] His first postwar play was produced at E. Martin Browne's and Robert Speaight's tiny (130 seats) Mercury Theatre on April 25, 1946, with Browne directing. Fry has said of Browne, "He has driven more poets to drama than any man living."[3] Their company was called The Pilgrim Players, after the wartime group with which Browne had worked. They not only revived such staples as Eliot's *Murder in the Cathedral*, but introduced in the London theater Fry's *Phoenix*, Anne Ridler's *The Shadow Factory*, Ronald Duncan's *This Way to the Tomb*, and Norman Nicholson's *The Old Man of the Mountains*. Although the impetus of the Mercury Theatre was primarily poetic as Browne has said ("I invited practicing poets to write verse in the form of a play . . .")[4] it was also an attempt to establish a professional religious theater that could play to commercial audiences. In this regard, Fry and Eliot were taking similar paths. As Fry has pointed out, dramatists,

> may learn something about the adaptability of style to subject and circumstance. The difference between *Murder in the Cathedral* and, say, *The Cocktail Party* is to some extent the difference between the Chapter House at Canterbury and a West End theatre.[5]

The success of Fry's adaptation is attested by the revival of *A Phoenix* at the Arts Theatre Club on November 20, 1946, followed by a run of sixty-four performances in the West End. Four years later it opened in New York in April, 1950, at the Fulton, but it was withdrawn after only five performances, largely because of faulty acting and its awkward coupling with a racial play called *Freight*.

Fry tells us that the title of *A Phoenix* comes from Robert Burton quoting Martial,

> *To whom conferr'd a peacock's undecent,*
> *A squirrel's harsh, a phoenix too frequent.*

Later he remarks that *Venus Observed* "was planned as one of a series of four comedies, a comedy for each of the seasons of the year, four comedies of mood. . . . The scene, the season and the characters are bound together in one climate." [6] *Venus Observed* is autumnal and *The Dark is Light Enough*, wintry; *The Lady's not for Burning*, he tells us elsewhere, is representative of the mood of spring. When he wrote *A Phoenix*, he had not yet begun to label his comedies by season, but it is set on a summer's night. For the miniature plot, "The story was got from Jeremy Taylor who had it from Petronius," [7] Fry tells us. An Ephesian matron had sworn to starve herself to death in her husband's tomb, but was persuaded to change her mind by the pleas of a handsome young corporal of the guard. While Petronius had ridiculed the attempt to substitute platonic love for sexual passion, Taylor uses the same story to stress the golden mean: one extreme leads to another. Fry, for his part, celebrates the ecstatic triumph of the Life Force over the instincts of self-destruction.

The gap between *The Boy* and *A Phoenix* is large, but it should not be exaggerated. With *Phoenix* Fry has followed episodic by focused plot, religious by secular play. But if anything, *A Phoenix* is even more mythic, more archetypal than *The Boy* or even *The Firstborn* which Fry was still working on. As Eliot has said of himself by indirection in his famous 1923 *Dial* review, Joyce in *Ulysses* was "manipulating a continuous parallel between contemporaneity and antiquity," although "the immense panorama of futility and anarchy which is contemporary history" becomes Fry's setting rather than the content which he dramatizes. Although Fry constructs his plays deliberately, he does not consciously select his "sources." When questioned about his literary predecessors, he commented:

> Is it possible to say where and how a young writer will find his elders' work of use to him? Different men will help themselves differently from what they read or see in performance. . . . To be sure of "influence" is always difficult. They work underground.[8]

In adopting Taylor's version of Petronius' story of sexual intrigue, he has taken up a myth with an ancient and widespread appeal. Nearly fifty years before, J. M. Synge had heard the same tale on his first visit to the Aran Isles in 1898. Synge used the plot for *In the Shadow of the Glen* in 1903. Even remote China has a similar tale, F. L. Lucas has discovered,[9] and the story has been used by writers as diverse as Chapman in *The Widow's Tears* (1612), Molière in *The Imaginary Invalid* (1673), and Voltaire in *Zadig* (1747). La Fontaine's *La Matrone D'Ephese* (1682) ends with the phrase, "Mieux vout goujat debout qu' Empereur enterré" (Better a flunky on two feet than an emperor in the grave).

Without consciously intending it, Fry hit upon a myth which embodies the desire of mankind for choice, despite the apparent inevitability of an unwanted and unchosen death. Jennet's dilemma between death at the stake or a degrading seduction in *The Lady*, the Duke of Altair's choice between nearly identical mistresses followed by

Perpetua's alternatives of submission to the Duke and death by burning in V*enus*, and Gettner's quandary between loss of identity and a meaningless execution at the end of *The Dark* all pose variants of the same problem. As Freud has analyzed it, choice stands in the place of necessity, of destiny. Where in reality man obeys compulsion, in myth he exercises choice, taking not a thing of horror (death) but the most desirable thing in life (love). For Jung the pattern which appears in A *Phoenix* and through much of the rest of Fry's writing is the "archetype of transformation," a continuity of symbols expressing the disintegration and death of the old pattern and the gradual emergence of a new order.

The setting for the play is "An underground tomb, in darkness except for a very low light of an oil-lamp. Above ground the starlight shows a line of trees on which hang the bodies of several men." The tomb, crosses, and imminent dawn of a third day spent with a corpse all carry Christian overtones. Moreover, while the world above is a commonsense, probable world of zoning laws and deathly conformity, the world below is erotic and wonderful—a dreamlike refuge from hostility and loneliness. Each level is counterpointed against the other.

Like the clever servants in Restoration comedy, Doto, who is awaiting death with her mistress Dynamene, is opportunistic, sceptical and sensual. She tries to keep up the conventional pretense of seriousness and virtue, but she can't keep men out of her mind even if she were so inclined. "It's a kind of stammer in my way of life," the sound of her name revealing her character. As confidante, she is as earthy as Dynamene is idealistic, her good-natured frankness emphasizing the perverse guilt which underlies Dynamene's dedication. "Life is more big than a bed / And full of miracles and mysteries like / One man made for one woman, etcetera, etcetera."

Dynamene, the most complex character in the play, is torn between a compelling death wish and her sensuous involvement in life. She unconsciously feels guilty for not having treated her husband Virilius better, and frustrated because he had been incapable of fulfilling her desires. Both Petronius and Taylor stress the widow's inordinate grief, but Fry sees in it a masochistic attempt to exorcise guilt-feelings. Dynamene tries to praise her dead spouse, but slips into burlesque. "You were the peroration of nature," she says, but in life, she quickly—if inadvertently—reveals, he had been stodgy, unimaginative, and dry, an uninspired pedant. A drudging civil servant, notable mostly for penmanship and punctuality, Virilius (despite his name "virility") was a cold lover, who made love as he kept books, mechanically and routinely: his voice made "Balance sheets sound like Homer and Homer sound / Like balance sheets." She had taught him, she says, "In your perceptive moments to appreciate me." Yet in her single-mindedness the widow fails to see how intimately involved in life her dedication to death is.

> What a mad blacksmith creation is
> Who blows his furnaces until the stars fly upward
> And iron Time is hot and politicians glow
> And bulbs and roots sizzle into hyacinth
> And orchis, and the sand puts out the lion,
> Roaring yellow, and oceans bud with porpoises,
> Blenny, tunny and the almost unexisting
> Blindfish; throats are cut, the masterpiece
> Looms out of labour; nations and rebellions
> Are spat out to hang on the wind—and all is gone
> In one Virilius, wearing his office tunic
> Checking the pence column as he went.

Now she carries her guilt at having somehow failed Virilius to the point of suicide, yet her outlook is ambivalent. "When the thoughts would die, the instincts will set sail / For life. And when the thoughts are alert for life / The instincts will rage to be destroyed on the rocks."

Attracted by the light, the young soldier guarding the hanged criminals enters the tomb. A brusque (to Doto) incompetent, he is named Tegeus (from the Latin *tegere*, "to cover," as the widow says of his name, "That's very thin for you. / It hardly covers your bones"). Virilius, Tegeus, Doto, and Dynamene may correspond somewhat ironically to Empire, Heroism, Love, and Pride, respectively, like a similar quartet, according to Shaw, in *The Simpleton of the Unexpected Isles* (and also in *Heartbreak House*, according to Shaw's biographer, Archibald Henderson). Tegeus gossips rather fraternally with Doto, shivers queasily at their companionable suttee and guilelessly ridicules the seriousness of his duties.

> Now they hang
> About at the corner of the night, they're present
> And absent, horribly obsequious to every
> Move in the air, and yet they keep me standing
> For five hours at a stretch.

Bored by her abstinence and preoccupied with sex, Doto tries to seduce Tegeus. But he is too shy, too impressed with Dynamene's "loyalty, enduring passion, / Unrecking bravery and beauty all in one." Paradoxically, although he is inspired by the widow's "human integrity" to announce his "renewed faith in human nature," he perceives he must himself become the object of her ideals in order to save her.

Yet once Tegeus has been captivated by Dynamene, whose name means "power," he finds himself in an untenable middle way. She may either reject him, intensifying his shyness, or rededicate herself to self-destruction, nipping his nascent self-confidence in the bud. However, with her over-sexed competitor asleep, Dynamene flirts, then resists Tegeus' responses. Finally she accepts Tegeus' attempts to redirect her attention from death back to life. "The earth's / Daylight would be my grave if I had left you / In that unearthly night," he says.

Their *cortesia*, or game of passion, not only diverts their interests from physical, outward quests to spiritual journeys inward and back into the past, but into the innocence of childhoods together. Like the mythic quester who restores fertility to a wasteland laid sterile by the impotence of its King, Tegeus resurrects from Dynamene's soul a spiritual "fountain of confidence / When the world is arid." Dynamene's new name for him, Chromis or "color," suggests the emergence of his true character from shyness, while its "bread-like sound" together with his wine, drunk in the memory of Virilius, bring together old master and new, Virilius and Chromis, the sacrament and Christ. By sharing Tegeus' bread and wine in a sacramental spirit, they mystically heal with love the "sickness" of alienation which had infected their world, "an oval twirling blasphemy." The very love which had made Dynamene attempt suicide now becomes the source of her renewal: she has realized that life will not renounce her.

Their passionate attachment rises to an ecstasy of desire when Tegeus suddenly recalls his guard duty and leaves to check his "boys," while Doto—now an embarrassing intruder—awakes. Desperately trying to get rid of Doto both to consummate her love in private and to avoid ridicule, the widow finally insists. Doto leaves, passing the now shocked and distraught Tegeus on the stairs. Relatives had cut down one of the criminals for burial. According to "section six, paragraph / Three in the Regulations," he must take the place of the missing man.[10] Tegeus threatens suicide, but is saved by Dynamene's revived wit: Virilius, not Tegeus, shall be hung in the criminal's place, allowing Tegeus in turn to replace Virilius. Tegeus has lost a body and returned to find true love, a comic reversal of Dynamene's awakening earlier to find a corpse after her earlier dream of love. And Doto's drinking to both masters simultaneously—the one who died under the curse of the law and the one who lives—is the very heart of the play: "The Master. Both the masters." Through Virilius, the ironic "virility" of his name has been fulfilled, for through him has come the resurrection of all the characters.

Despite the coincidental meeting, apparent doom and fortuitous solution, the characters' fates are not imposed but arise from their own traits. Had Tegeus not been impressionable, naïve, lonely, and idealistic, he would never have investigated the tomb, stayed in defiance of decorum, or taken both Dynamene's self-sacrifice or the consequences of the loss of a hanged criminal at face value. And Dynamene's powers of rationalization, passion, and loyalty put her in the tomb at the beginning and get both Tegeus and herself out of it at the end with a clear conscience.

The style of *A Phoenix* carries over most of the traits of Fry's idiom in *The Boy*: the internal rhymes, a penchant for all kinds of alliteration and assonance, contained within a highly auditory, rhythmic blank verse. Gone, however, are the chorus and with it, the convention of assigning verse to the highborn and prose to buffoons. Now all the characters speak poetry, a highly contrived and brilliantly artificial verse as it must be. The high quality of Fry's language goes far to disprove Eliot's axiom that following the Jacobeans, blank verse lost its usefulness to drama. It is not the rhythms, but the diction which must be revitalized. Fry has used all kinds of punning inversions ("such a stern prow / Such a proud stern"), balanced antitheses ("To be a coming man / Already gone"), and a knack for pyramiding phrases, each longer than the one preceding, each modifying a central idea in a different direction.

> *throats are cut, the masterpiece,*
> *Looms out of labour; nations and rebellions*
> *Are spat out to hang on the wind.*

At the same time, the surface texture is extremely rich and dense, fleshed out with a plethora of totally appropriate classical allusion, witty imagery often joining unlike qualities in a striking metaphysical conjunction, curiosities of flora and fauna ("blenny, tunny and the almost unexisting / Blindfish"), and proper names. Fry is particularly adept at epithet-chopping, the deliberate use of inflated rhetoric to burlesque the inconsequential.

> *I swear the hypnotic oath, by all the Titans—*
> *By Koeos, Krios, Iapetos, Kronos, and so on—*
> *By the three Hekatoncheires, by the insomnia*
> *Of Tisiphone, by Jove, and the dew*
> *On the feet of my boyhood.*

He also deflates false transports of emotion by inserting banalities, as when Dynamene and Tegeus repeat the names of scented things: "parsley . . . Seaweed . . . Lime trees . . . Fruit in the fire"; Doto interjects, "Horses." Deliberate phrasal anachronisms are used as when Doto drinks, "One for the road," characters speak in music-hall fashion at complete cross-purposes, and rapid changes of tone occur bathetically. It may occur within a single speech, as when Doto unsuccessfully resists the temptation to eat. "I'll turn my back on you. It means utter / Contempt. Eat? Utter contempt. Oh, little new rolls!"

Once Dynamene and Tegeus-Chromis actually fall in love, most of the farcical pyrotechnics end and the verse becomes more serious in tone, although humor still appears. Differences between Dynamene's rhetoric and Tegeus' are more a matter of degree than of kind, but hers tends toward the romantically evocative: "a cold bell sounding in a golden month." Tegeus tends toward the more loftily philosophical and epigrammatic:

> for however long
> I may be played by this poor musician, existence,
> Your person and sacrifice will leave their trace
> As clear upon me as the shape of the hills
> Around my birthplace.

As Dynamene says, Tegeus "falls easily into superlatives." In *A Phoenix* Fry has fashioned a marvelously idiomatic poetic language which manages to be fully contemporary and witty without losing either its depths of meaning or its flexibility on the lips of his players.

In *A Phoenix* Fry has written his most impressive play, compressing within its brief scope an enormous range of philosophical, supernatural, and human complexities. Of all his drama it comes closest to his ideal play "which would be both the immediate appearance of things and the eternal nature of things, combined with felicity." [11] The play's symbolism is effectively embodied in its metaphorical chiaroscuro of day and night, death and life, demonstrating the resurrection of love, the Phoenix, from its ashes and new love from a dead husband's corpse. Fry has also managed to make the fullest use of all the deeply founded insights of symbolism, both Christian and pagan, which he has drawn on throughout his career. Thus *A Phoenix* is Fry's most symmetrical, best-constructed, most tightly unified play. In its formal dialectic, its balanced oppositions and counterpointed gesture, it attains the coherence and beauty of dance.

5

The Lady's not for Burning

The Lady's not for Burning,[1] Fry's first full-length comedy, is his best-known and most controversial play. As Fry has recalled, "the play which first gave rise to the bacchic figure vomiting his careless words, was five or six months finding its shape before writing began, and eight months in writing." Fry had sent the play to John Gielgud who was puzzled by it, but pressed his backers to take up production rights. At the Arts Theatre Club where it opened in March, 1948, with Gielgud and Pamela Brown (by Fry's stipulation) in the leading roles, *The Lady* carried off the Shaw Prize Fund for best play of the year. After touring the provinces for eight weeks, it reopened for eight months at London's Globe Theatre. Then the production moved to New York, where it opened at the Royale Theatre, November 8, 1950, going on there for another long and successful run.

The Lady is the first of Fry's seasonal comedies, a comedy of mood.

> I have tried to make the words and the deeds of the characters move all the time with a sense of the particular moment at which they are said or done, so that we can be aware continually of the April afternoon, for example, with the scents and sounds of it, or of the April evening and night as the play goes on: moreover, to make these scents and sounds an essential part of the action, conditioning the words of the characters . . .[2]

Then too, in a headnote Fry has included the words of a convict who had confessed falsely to a murder, February

1947. "In the past I wanted to be hung. It was worth while being hung to be a hero, seeing that life was not really worth living." The title itself, while summing up the outcome, may glance at Paul's words in I Corinthians 7:9—"It is better to marry than to burn" (either with lust or at the stake).

As a conscious elaboration of a master theme and mood, *The Lady* overlaps Fry's other, earlier work. His flamboyant, impulsive verbal bravura has blossomed into a brilliance which only the full-length comic form could adequately display. From *The Firstborn* Fry has carried over the reality-illusion conflict, the theme of social and cosmological disorder, and an atmosphere of mystery. Like Dynamene in *A Phoenix*, Thomas Mendip is a death-seeker whose interest, no matter how sincere, must be shifted to love of, and to Life. And Jennet, like Tegeus is rescued by love from an arbitrary death sentence whose reality is attested by the instruments of death (the hanging tree, the stake) which form the background.

In many respects *The Lady* has drawn upon the conventions of the comedy of manners which arose after the Restoration with Etherege, Wycherley, Dryden and others, reached the peak of its brilliance in Congreve's *The Way of the World*, spluttered again into life with Sheridan's two remarkable comedies and then lapsed. After over a century, it reappeared in Wilde, most notably in *Lady Windermere's Fan* and *The Importance of Being Earnest*. Fry's *The Lady* also has its gay and serious couples, its quarreling brothers, a benevolent Lady Bountiful type, a pedantic chaplain, avaricious justice of the peace, befuddled mayor, adolescent foundling, and comic "low life" ragpicker. As usual, the play develops farcically, when Jennet is confused with a witch in the toils of Thomas, the devil, with its eavesdropping scene, the rake Humphrey's attempted seduction of Jennet, the rapid changes of possible marital partners, and even a short proviso scene. In the end, two shrewd young women catch two clever but reluctant young men who have been their destined spouses throughout the play.

Nearer our own time Thomas Mendip, like Lord Darlington in Wilde's *Lady Windermere's Fan*, belongs to the society he criticizes. Mendip also resembles Dick Dudgeon of Shaw's *The Devil's Disciple*; and Jennet Jourdemain, like Shaw's Saint Joan, is a girlish, innocent type as firmly committed to the everyday as Joan is on fire with God. And in *The Lady* as in *Man and Superman*, Thomas Mendip and John Tanner are—in a sense—brilliant gasbags who adopt the devil's advocacy to deflate social pretensions, only to be punctured and domesticated by versions of Everywoman.

Because *The Lady* is so complicated and diverse, critics have applied such terms as "symphonic" to its apparently nonprogressive plot, and Fry himself has termed it "first cousin to an artificial comedy." Nevertheless, the strands of the plot can be separated. In the main plot, as Fry has described it, the careers of Thomas and Jennet form a kind of 'X': they "start by having two opposing views of life; they end by fusing them and creating a third view." Thomas receives from Jennet an acceptance of love and life, while he converts her rationalism to a sense of mystery, granting both a tolerance of human complexity and ambiguity which neither before had glimpsed. The action of the "gay couple" is counterpointed wittily by a "serious couple" in the subplot, as in Restoration comedy. Alizon Eliot begins by getting her man, the foundling Richard (perhaps taken from Wilde's *The Importance of Being Earnest*), and ends by setting them both free. Jennet begins by seeking her freedom and ends by getting her man. At the same time, the twins Humphrey and Nicholas Devize complicate the action by casting doubt on the credibility of Thomas' murder and competing first for Alizon and then for Jennet. Thus they place the idealized passions of both "gay" and "serious" couples within the perspective of real life, with its lusts, violence, and lies.

Fry's comedy thus appears to uphold a civilized norm against the individual's willful departure from it, while he wishes, as Spears suggests, "to make custom, convention, common sense, and worldly wisdom ridiculous, to redeem joy from its low companions and associate it with the spiritual and idealistic." [3] Yet Fry has avoided the sentimental denial of the existence of evil which Spears and others seem to find in the play by creating a double perspective. When Thomas and Jennet hold the stage, through their passionate energy, their delight in the world, and their witty expression, they appear to be "vital" characters. They are seemingly victimized by the constricted, "artificial" System embodied in the ruling establishment of Cool Clary, a backward and superstitious medieval English town. To the well-meaning but obtuse mayor, the urbanely incompetent magistrate and the scatterbrained but practical Margaret, Thomas is an obsessed "humour" character. Since he appears to repeat his fixation—"though we administer persuasion . . . the man / Won't stop admitting"—society must either expel or hang him (as he wishes) or include him, projecting the action forward toward the scenes of discovery and reconciliation.

Despite the conventions which Fry has taken over from the Restoration comedians and their successors, he has more in common with Chekhov and Shaw than he does with Congreve and Sheridan. For Thomas Mendip, with his comic existentialism, does not function as *either* a ridiculer *or* reflector; it is a case of *both / and*. Man's pretensions to immortality, self-love, and beauty are mocked as Thomas says,

> *I defend myself against pain and death by pain*
> *And death, and make the world go round, they tell me,*
> *By one of my less lethal appetites;*
> *Half this grotesque life I spend in a state*
> *Of slow decomposition, using*
> *The name of unconsidered God as a pedestal*
> *On which I stand and bray that I'm best*
> *Of beasts, until under some patient*
> *Moon or other I fall to pieces.*

But the futility of Thomas' fury is also stressed. The extraordinary vigor, clarity, and intelligence with which Thomas attacks his own vices only strengthen our sense that he is helpless to mitigate their power over him.

In the first act Thomas Mendip, a slightly drunk, dis-
charged soldier, confronts a young clerk in the house of
Cool Clary's mayor with a demand that he be hanged. He
has come into the medieval room from a light kind of
Renaissance set in "1400 either more or less or exactly."
Like Pirandello and Anouilh, Fry has invented a fairy-tale
world to win our consent to his ideas, mixing in enough
reality to hold our belief, with enough fantasy to have us
accept Thomas' sincerity. Mendip's murder is as fictitious
as that of Synge's Playboy, and he is at least partly motivated—as we later learn—by a desire to save an innocent
"witch" from lynching. But his death wish is genuine
enough, arising mostly from his stint as a soldier demanding expiation.

> I've been unidentifiably
> Floundering in Flanders for the past seven years,
> Prising open ribs to let men go
> On the indefinite leave which needs no pass.

Thomas is filled with loathing by the sheer messiness,
the untidiness of existence. What oppresses him is the
decay of the body, and his imagination consequently is
fixed upon images of nauseous smells, sensations of sticki-
ness, poisonous gropings.

> Flesh weighs like a thousand years, and every morning
> Wakes heavier for an intake of uproariously
> Comical dreams which smell of henbane.
> Guts, humours, ventricles, nerves, fibres
> And fat—the arterial labyrinth, body's hell.

Every object and every event he experiences seems, in its
sheer arbitrariness, to imply that the kind of metaphysical
order he craves is an impossibility.

> What guile recommends the world
> And gives our eyes the special sense to be
> Deluded, above all animals?

In his consuming disgust, Thomas would live the incorpo-
real life of the unconscious dead, being no longer a man
but a senseless being "sleep[ing] it off in a stupor of

dust / Till the morning after the day of judgment." Although like Cymen in *Thor, with Angels*, he struggles persistently against the regenerating power of Life, his pessimism does not preclude his delight in the world or in palpable metaphor.

Next to appear is "the little blonde religious," Alizon Eliot, for her arranged marriage to Humphrey Devize, the mayor's nephew. She, together with the foundling Richard, are the play's "serious couple." They fall in love passionately and sentimentally. As lovers their naturalness and, at the end, their fiery spirit, help them avoid some of the triteness of the conventional affair. Yet the difficulties lying between them and marriage place the similar impossibility of Thomas' execution—"sweet pretty noose, nice noose"—in a wryly humorous light. Thus, from the beginning, Fry has divided his characters not so much into T. S. Eliot's sensitive and insensitive, or as some of his critics have supposed, into "marvellers and nonmarvellers," but into those who can and those who cannot love life.

However, the growing passion of the two, punctuated by Thomas' witty sallies, is interrupted by the entrance of Nicholas Devize, Humphrey's twin brother. He threatens Richard (after supposedly killing Humphrey) with a farcical *miles gloriosus* attack.

> But I was conceived as a hammer,
> And born in a rising wind. . . . I'm the receipt God
>   followed
> In the creation. It took the roof off his oven.

The mock-resurrection of Humphrey is pure Bergson: an element of the mechanical encrusted on the living. The puncture of Nicholas' "confession" by Humphrey's revival not only mocks Thomas' ploy, but also anticipates the return of *his* victim, the ragpicker Skipps. It also suggests that underlying sexual passion is a powerful impulse toward chaotic, disorganizing violence, as Freud has made clear.

The Devize twins harken back to the eighteenth-century comic rakes who, beginning with Farquhar and Goldsmith, hunted brides by pairs in the country. Both lecherous, mercurial, and combative, they are slightly differentiated. Nicholas is a well-intentioned, ineffectual youth, contrasting with his brother Humphrey, a loutish, hardheaded, and rather likable villain. The dizzying speed with which their passions are born, grow, and die, is played off against the outworn social conventions of arranged marriages, thievery by legal process, and condemnation by mob protest.

Jennet Jourdemain then enters, fleeing an enraged, superstitious mob who suspect her of witchcraft. Like Hoel in *Thor* she is accused of misusing supernatural powers; also like Hoel, she wants to live. "Where do I lodge my application?" A beautiful, slightly eccentric, commonsense young lady, she is self-characterized: "I believe in the human mind . . . the daughter / Of a man who believed the universe was governed / By certain laws." Her solemn idealism is played off against Thomas' furious reformism, her appeals for cool reason against the mayor's covert—and the mob's overt—blood lust.

> *What, does everyone still knuckle*
> *And suckle at the big breast of irrational fears? . . .*
> *Can they think and then think like this?*

Mayor Tyson finds himself inexplicably trapped in a situation demanding a rite of exorcism instead of the routine prayers he had expected. Against his will and habit, he is forced to conduct a bogus trial, forcing upon the defendants verdicts exactly opposite to that desired by them: Jennet is to be burned, while Thomas is to be denied hanging. Entering to confuse the issue with facts, a comically ineffectual chaplain reports a rumor that Jennet has transformed Thomas' supposed victim into a dog. A key to the theme, he finds life a perpetual miracle.

> *But life has such*
> *Diversity, I sometimes remarkably lose*
> *Eternity in the passing moment.*

All the other characters present differing versions of the same situation, permitting Thomas to cover his tracks: he announces histrionically, "The Last Trump / Is timed for twenty-two forty hours precisely." Because Jennet's beauty, freshness, and fantastic stories have so "enchanted" and "charmed" her listeners, she is adjudged an "enchantress bemused into collaboration with the enemy of man"—with Thomas in his role of devil's advocate; both are then led off for questioning.

By playing off Jennet's romantic visions against Thomas' grotesque apocalyptic view, Fry lays bare the common impracticality of both legal process and martyrdom within a disturbed, chaotic society. Both victims are ostensibly criminals looking for a crime which is seeking them in turn, both attacking society's "brainstorm of absurdities." Yet she is condemned while Thomas is just as arbitrarily disbelieved. By contrasting one irrational law—where there's magic there must be witches—with another—where there's guilt there's crime—Fry keeps the main emphasis on the protagonists. He also keeps alive the possibility of redemption for the village itself.

The second act involves two forward impulses. One is the unraveling, which evens out the disparities in knowledge which had existed at the beginning of the play so that at the end everyone knows everything. The second, overlapping movement, emancipation, creates from the breakdown of the old social order a new social order. While the first act had placed the initiative for revelation and change in the hands of a group of energetic but confused youths, the second act restores it to their more conservative elders—whose methods, ironically, are far less enlightened. Committed to a restoration of convention and dull routine, they struggle with difficulty to cope with annoying emergencies, rioting, and cosmic disorder. "The street's gone mad. They've seen a shooting star!" Their whole petty universe seems to be collapsing, along with their moral values, unstrung by Jennet's wealth and beauty.

Ironically, the chaplain suggests that Thomas be forcibly "wooed" from death by happiness, joining Alizon's prenuptial party. In this way a civilized-norm will overcome Thomas' misanthropic departures from it. One of Fry's best creations, the chaplain's "feeling" contrasts with the others' "thought," his wonder at existence with Thomas' obsessed naturalism: he sometimes loses "eternity in the passing moment." His real love being music, he is even more uncomfortable in the practical world than in dogmatic theology. "All my friends tell me I actually exist / And by an act of faith I have come to believe them."

Forced to reprimand first the Devize brothers for trying to seduce Jennet, and then Richard for surly rebellion, the Mayor and Justice plan to eavesdrop on Thomas and Jennet to gather more evidence. Since their authority is virtually unchallenged anyway, the advice is largely a contrivance to bring back Thomas and Jennet.

> A *hypothetical Devil, Tappercoom,*
> *Brought into conversation with a witch.*
> A *dialogue of Hell, perhaps, and conclusive.*
> *Or one or other by their exchange of words*
> *Will prove to be innocent, or we shall have proof*
> *Positive of guilt.*

Sheridan's use of the device in *The School for Scandal* seems far better motivated, with its fast-paced revelations and comic reversals.

Like the long tête à tête between Dynamene and Tegeus in *A Phoenix*, the debate between Thomas and Jennet rolls together overtones of a legal trial, a game of passion, and ritual conversion as their roles multiply and shift. While Jennet has (unwillingly) been cast as witch, martyr, and nun, Thomas zestfully plays *advocatus diaboli*, confessor, and mock-lover. Just as he had unsuccessfully tried to wring a hanging sentence out of the mayor, he now attacks Jennet's grip on life—a satiric version of the visit of the disguised Duke to the condemned Claudio in *Measure for Measure*: "Thou hast nor youth nor age / But, as it were, an after dinner's sleep / Dreaming on both" (III, 1, 32–34). Only through laughter, an "irrelevancy / Which almost amounts to revelation" can she mollify contradictions. Although man's brutality, "the howl of human jackals," is surrounded by beauty, nature is indifferent.

> A *glittering smear, the snail trail of the sun*
> *Where it crawled with its golden shell into the hills.*
> A *darkening land sunken into prayer.*

Attacking the self-deception Jennet shares with all society, Thomas plays devil to her saint. Like the existentialist Orestes in Sartre's *The Flies*, he finds order and sensuous beauty in the universe no argument for some divinely-ordained moral purpose. While Thomas' self-destructive glimpses of human depravity fail to supplant his sensuous apprehension of natural wonders, Jennet wants to live without poetic vision. Piqued by her tenacious hold on the "essential fact," Thomas rejects Jennet's logical positivism for "creation's vast exquisite dilemma".

> *We have wasted paradox and mystery on you*
> *When all you ask us for, is cause and effect!*

Once Jennet impresses Thomas as a living, sensitive human being rather than a mere oppressed victim, their roles are reversed: he plays Adam to her Eve. She has exposed his violent exasperation and inflation as despair at his loss of a social, publicly acceptable persona: a local habitation and a name.

The eavesdroppers suddenly enter, having mistaken Jennet's Blakean inversions as a confession of witchcraft. "You are evil, Hell, the father of life; if so / Hell is my home and my days of good were a holiday." Fry makes striking use here of the well-made *quiproquo* (an over-heard conversation variously misunderstood). Thomas is reduced to impotent rage.

> *She has bribed you to procure*
> *Her death! Graft! Graft! Oh, the corruption*
> *Of this town when only the rich can get to kingdom*
> *Come and a poor man is left to groan*
> *In the full possession of his powers. And she's*
> *Not even guilty! I demand fair play*
> *For the criminal classes!*

In a farcical sequence of mischances Thomas knocks Humphrey down and threatens the chaplain with his viol, only to be cut short by Jennet, who faints. Chastened, he meekly consents to "spend the evening joyously" but only if Jennet also shares in the "awful festivity." Contrived as it may seem, Fry has revived the ancient tradition of including as many characters as possible in the comic festival centering around discovery (both of Thomas' "victim" and of "truth," in the larger sense) and reconciliation, both between and within characters.

In Act III the dismal, offstage prenuptial party (marred by Alizon's apparent desertion) is suddenly enlivened for the bored suitors by Jennet's theatrical entrance, "bright with jewels, and twenty years exquisitely out of fashion" (abetted by the maternal Margaret Devize). Condemned herself, Jennet ironically symbolizes the others' potential escape from convention and deadly monotony. Secure in both her new wonder at life and the apparent imminence of death, she gently ridicules Thomas' death wish, lays bare the nostalgic regret beneath the mayor's stuffiness ("I rustle with his memories!") and tactfully reconciles the quarreling twins. As Samuel Johnson has quipped, a fixed time of death concentrates the mind wonderfully.

After an interlude of confession, forcing Tappercoom to stiffen up both the tearful chaplain and mayor, Richard and Alizon finally lay bare their mutual passion. "We're lovers in a deep and safe place / And never lonely any more." As they plan to run away, Humphrey initiates a gross, sexual parody of Thomas' earlier, more symbolic ploy as this time, Thomas eavesdrops farcically. "You mean you give me a choice? / To sleep with you, or tomorrow to sleep with my fathers." As her hesitation excites Humphrey nearly to orgasm, his pleading neatly inverts the Bergsonian formula: Humphrey becomes something living encrusted on the mechanical. But he is so circumspect, so euphemistic, that his depravity is hard to take seriously.

While Nicholas pounds in the cellar where the escaping Richard has locked him, Thomas enters as mock *diabolus ex machina,* a spectacular response to Jennet's plea, "O God, I wish / The ground would open." Finally driven to confess he loves Jennet, he faces her gentle ridicule.

> My heart, my mind
> Would rather burn. But may not the casting vote
> Be with my body? And is the body necessarily
> Always ill-advised?

She now sees that Thomas, caught by pride, confusion, and sympathy, had invented a murder to save her.

> There was a soldier,
> Discharged and centreless, with a towering pride
> In his sensibility, and an endearing
> Disposition to be a hero, who wanted
> To make an example of himself to all
> Erring mankind, and falling in with a witch-hunt
> His good heart took the opportunity
> Of providing a diversion.

To the extent that Jennet's realization brings about her final choice of Thomas, resolving her fate, her comment can stand. But as a summary of Thomas' character, it is an intrusion better developed by action.

Richard and Alizon then return from their attempted elopement, bringing back Jennet's supposed "victim," old Skipps "because nobody now / Will be able to burn her." His appearance provides a mock-epiphany, a parodied "discovery" of the slain god placed by Cornford, Murray, and the Cambridge anthropologists at the climax of the ancient vegetation rites. As a drunken male malaprop— "immersion upon us miserable offenders"—who parodies the liturgy, Skipps both fulfills and mocks Thomas' apocalyptic visions. A drunken, stinking "corpse" who "floats in the heaven of the grape," he is a fool in a wise situation, the chaplain's ironic double, whose "resurrection" completes the death of the others' illusions.

With Jennet cleared, Thomas reluctantly agrees to postpone his death.

> Do you see those roofs and spires?
> There sleep hypocrisy, porcous pomposity, greed,
> Lust, vulgarity, cruelty, trickery, sham

> *And all possible nitwittery—are you suggesting fifty*
> *Years of that?*

Despite his love for Jennet, who "was only suggesting fifty / Years of me," he refuses to stop insisting that men are not angels, that they belong not to any unhistorical heaven of pure essences, but to the moving, restless world of existential time and space. "When the landscape goes to seed, the wind is obsessed / By tomorrow."

Thomas has received from Jennet the will to live, while she has accepted from him conversion to the riddle of mystery. Yet life is both miraculous and miserable; one can hardly come to terms with it without irony. As Mandel suggests, there is no victory over evil in the play because evil has not been defeated; it is endured for the sake of love. That society, as represented by Cool Clary, has room for an accomplished rogue like old Skipps but must expel its shrewdest, most vital critics, indicates another irony. This kind of group lacks the openness Bergson posits for the resolution of most comedy. As Johan Huizinga points out in *Homo Ludens: Man at Play,* society has always been more tolerant of its cheats than of its spoilsports, for its cheats at least pretend to obey the rules.

To emphasize Thomas' anti-messianic point, Fry has planted hints of the Christian mythos throughout the play. And Nelvin Vos has uncovered most of them in his essay on "The Comic Victim-Victor."

Thomas is a humorous Christic figure. The three main events of the play are mythic representations of significant events in the Christian view of history. The first, the fall of man, takes place in the garden. The "devil" (Humphrey) is temporarily defeated, but he is not really dead, and will be back in the second event, Christ's redemption. When Jennet is just ready to succumb to the "devil's" lures, Thomas appears to say she is not for burning. But the charges are not actually dismissed until the appearance of the resurrected Skipps. Thus, the Fall, the Redemption and Resurrection are comically represented in the play.

In a smaller context, the main characters and their

actions resemble Jesus' trial. The central character wants
to be hanged. He announces the Last Trump, and comes
to a civil magistrate (Pilate) with his eccentric wish.
Margaret (Pilate's wife) is fretfully uneasy. The Mayor's
indecisiveness leads to a scheme produced by a political
crony (Herod) and a religious figure (Caiaphas). The
three conspire until Thomas is called "Evil, Hell, the
Father of Lies," a comic inversion of the Son of God.
Thomas offers out of love to die and in the end, through
the resurrection of Skipps, is given a new life.

The language of *The Lady* has been attacked as indeco-
rous and glittery, but this is its whole point. Only to the
extent that Fry is able to give the play a fairy-tale atmosphere can the happy ending be made to appear plausible,
and his verse is a willing accomplice in this effort. When
the plot is being tightened or loosened—traps laid, attacks
launched or repulsed, alliances being formed or dissolved—the language has an admirable tautness.

NICHOLAS   As things turn out
    I want to commit an offence.
THOMAS   Does something prevent you?
NICHOLAS   I don't know what offence to commit.
THOMAS   What abysmal
    Poverty of mind!

Primarily, however, the speeches are rather extended,
more a series of lyrics which evoke moods rather than
forwarding the action with highly responsive dialogue.
Close examination justifies the summary Pallette has
made of its character.

> a spectacular melange of modern vulgate and exuberant
> hyperbole, indulging in rhetorical pyrotechnics, coining
> new words, linking together paradoxical elements, seeking a
> startling and new way of expression with a Dylan Thomas-
> like vividness.[4]

Along with overtones of Thomas appear wordplays remi-
niscent of Auden. "Sin, as well as God, / Moves in a most
mysterious way." There are witty puns characteristic of
Joyce ("turgidical"), and the consonantal mouthfuls of

abuse typical of O'Casey: "You slawsy poodle, you tike, / You crapulous puddering pip-squeak." The epigrammatic inversions of Wilde appear, and a Shavian stab: "I demand fair play for the criminal classes!" All these traits are typical of Mendip, whose boundless imagination is wittily reflected in his burlesques of the cosmic by the inconsequential, the vast by the insignificant.

> *Since opening time I've been*
> *Propped up at the bar of heaven and earth, between*
> *The wall-eye of the moon and the brandy-cask of the sun,*
> *Growling thick songs about jolly good fellows . . .*

Although all the characters have sprung unmistakably from Fry's pen, no one who has listened carefully to their speech could say they all sound alike. While Thomas' speech is distinguished by a restless, pervading irony, Jennet expresses no less wittily a childlike wonder and fancifulness.

> *If I try to find my way I bark my brain*
> *On shadows sharp as rocks where half a day*
> *Ago was a wild soft world, a world of warm*
> *Straw.*

While Tappercoom, like Thomas, "tempts providence with humour," he is more tolerant of human failings, speaking often in mild hyperbole, while the Devize twins are boastful and self-assertive. "Humphrey / Went twinkling like Lucifer into the daffodils." The mayor and his sister are humorless sources of humor in others and the chaplain contents himself with tiny jokes, mostly at his own expense.

Fry is also capable of impressive modulations of tone. In Thomas' angry attack on Tyson, a series of crabbed, obscure epithets ends climactically in a triplet of resounding monosyllables.

> *You bubble-mouthing, fog-blathering,*
> *Chin-chuntering, chap-flapping, liturgical,*
> *Turgidical, base old man.*

At other moments an oracular, meditative tone appears, as when Jennet argues:

> *Then sad was my mother's pain, sad my breath,*
> *Sad the articulations of my bones.*
> *Sad, sad my alacritous web of nerves,*
> *Woefully, woefully sad my wandering brain.*

The repetition of hissing consonants and moaning vowels suggests perfectly the painful tone of confession.

While it is true that the language sometimes halts the action, or may fail to bring about the revelations being analyzed, the witty associations are addressed to the awakened intelligence, projecting the play's meaning upon another dimension.

In the absence of any vital, all-pervading tradition of ideas in the contemporary theater or in social institutions, Fry has revived for dramatic purposes a set of interlocking or dovetailed conventions which reached their fullest development in the late Middle Ages. These motifs which form what Scott Buchanan calls the "analogical matrix" are alchemy, martyrdom and seduction. In alchemy the center of nature is eventually to be united with its circumference in the sun, as in Christianity the soul of man is ultimately united with its circumference in God, forming a symbolic association between the purifying of the human soul and the transmuting of the earth (or "base" metals) to gold. If we recall the metaphysical pun of "to die" on the sexual climax, the tendency of all the characters to view martyrdom as a stimulus or end to passion becomes clear enough. For Jennet and Thomas to be able to laugh at sin and error, like Chaucer's Troilus, means that they have surmounted them.

The evils of the play have appeared fantastic and unreal to some critics, who have objected to Thomas' phony murder, Jennet's unlikely punishment and the magistrate's silliness. To them the mystery appears under-dramatized and overstated. Yet the action of dark comedy like *The Lady*, as Northrop Frye has pointed out, often moves toward a deliverance from something which, if absurd, is by no means invariably harmless. Humphrey's concern that Jennet first consent to her rape does not conceal his lust, while on the other hand, Thomas' laughable extremism does not erase the absolute probability of human death or the distinct possibility of stupidly miscalculated mass-destruction.

Yet the fact that most of the characters are so deeply moved toward forgiveness by perilously artificial contrivances may strike us as untrue to real life. Their change in character seems inconsistent with the lusts, greed, and irrationality that lead to burnings, hangings, rapes, and war. Despite Fry's carefully sustained equilibrium between the real and the fantastic, the comic and the ironic, the reform of the blocking characters—the mayor, justice and Devize twins—along with the tacit assumption that the crowd hysteria will simply melt away, may strike an audience as overly sanguine and even sentimental, but these are matters of balance and perspective rather than flaws in the work.

If the play were a tragedy Thomas' views would result in the destruction of evil both in society and in himself. Since the play is tragicomedy, both Thomas and the evils he attacks are both significant and ridiculous, long-lasting and surmountable. It is typical of Fry that the commonplace for society (marriage) should become the wonderful for the idealists (love-at-first-sight) in the main and subordinate plots, while the probable for the idealists (sudden death) should become the marvelous (a witchhunt and burning) for society. The conclusion confirms another pattern in Fry: the women who stand at the dramatic center of his comic plots represent a "higher" love than his men achieve. The excessive concern with the bodily leads his "lower" characters into lust, avarice, and destruction; the vices are transposed into aspiration, self-sacrifice, and sublimation by his "higher" characters.

6

Thor, with Angels

Thor, with Angels,[1] presented in June as the Canterbury Festival play of 1948, is set a century or two before *The Boy*, on a Jutish farmstead, A.D. 596. The re-Christianization of England under Ethelbert, king of Kent, with its backdrop of incessant feuding among the transplanted Germanic tribes presents a ready-made parallel to the situation Europe finds itself in today: demoralized, self-destructive, and suspicious, but with enormous potential for transformation. *Thor* is still one more attempt by Fry to deal with the problem of how Christianity, now the half-forgotten faith of an embattled minority, is to be restored to a dominant spiritual position in society. For his protagonist, Fry has invented a mythic Jutish leader, Cymen of the Copse, who rejects the bloody, sacrificial Woden-worship as he gradually discovers God. As in *The Firstborn*, the death of an innocent young man fully enlightens him. A defeated warrior who is opposed by a muttering clan, he is at war within himself, attempting to reconcile his deepest instincts toward death with love of his fellow man.

For the only time in his plays, Fry reconstructs on the stage a modern version of the primal horde (albeit satirically), the primitive order of society which Freud has pieced together in *Totem and Taboo*. According to Freud the first social unit was familial and paternalistic: the father was a despotic tyrant who kept his sons subjected to his authority by the exercise of brute force, self-glorification, and a superior will. This led inevitably to his own violent death once his sons had become powerful enough to challenge his authority. It is Freud's theory that, to end chaos and instability, society invented religion, government, and the military, transferring the power of the father to their representatives: the priest, king, and general.

Although Freud's theory seems to have little historical validity, and Fry himself has spoken slightingly of those who have "burrowed with Freud," the pattern of *Thor* corresponds closely to Freud's hypothesis, with a key difference: under the impact of miraculous visions Cymen is overcome by the mystery of love rather than by his envious sons. Yet the divine intervenes so decisively, when Cymen intends to speak or do evil, that literal miracle takes on all the defects of the *deus ex machina*: incredibility and mechanical necessity. And although the minor characters are flat and undifferentiated, the crucifixion of the helpless Hoel reveals Freudian "displacement," the substitution of a representative or symbol for the feared and hated father. At the same time, Hoel's death satisfies the traditional Christian dogma of salvation through vicarious death. While the attack on Hoel by the brothers parallels Cymen's assault on Woden, the "lower" passions are transcended by the "higher," revenge by forgiveness.

Thor begins with a dishonored homecoming, as Cymen returns from battle with the Saxons. With him he has brought Hoel, a Briton slave of the Saxons whom Cymen has inexplicably saved from death on the battlefield. This is despite the fact that Hoel had killed Eccha, the Jutish earl, and deserves, as Cymen's brother-in-law Osmer puts it, "the joy of our vengeance and a shove / To doom and a damned journey into dust." By centering his action around the conflicts of Jute and Saxon, mercy and revenge, the play moves toward the establishment of a mystically-glimpsed ideal theocracy: "the men of Rome / Returning, bringing God, winter over, a breath / Of green exhaled from the hedges." Although the play deals with the tragic themes of man in a chaotic, incomprehensible world, a world which has nearly forgotten a god of mercy and remembers a god of blood savagery only too well, the inner action is organized along ironic lines. Fry has followed the invisible satirists, Swift and Shaw, playing off a vital, sceptical Ironist against the function-bound Imposters representing a deluded society, "rigid with reality." As Mandel points out, Cymen's household is meant to stand for law-abiding normalcy, that is, revenge, cruel gods, and primitive sacrifice. Their conventional decency is shocked and they are morally upset by the apparently malicious spirit of mercy that has bewitched Cymen.

QUICHELM   "Love one another";
     What a way to honour the gods!
CLODESUIDA   He's not himself.
     It is the patter of delirium he talks.

In a world where genocide is sanctioned by the supposed necessities of national survival, these frankly, openly evil pagans stand for modern man, and Cymen's mysterious pity represents a Christianity which is as yet a state of hope, rather than history.

Cymen's family all want him to sacrifice the Briton; when he refuses they consider him mad. Cymen's sons, Quichelm and Cheldric, and his brothers-in-law, Tadfrid and Osmer, are hostile, cruel and malicious, with a conservative behavior and attitude toward life. For his part Cymen is brusque, affectionate and witty, desperately trying to cover a confused anxiety with an exaggerated camaraderie. He wants to keep Hoel alive to find out what force is sapping his will, dissipating his strength into meditation. "You can tell me," he says to the captive,

> What flogged away my strength
> What furtive power in your possession
> pulled the passion of my sword. Name that devil!

But Hoel has forgotten—"The One God, he's called. But I can't remember the details"—and when the infuriated Cymen, spurred on by his relatives, makes to kill him, he finds his sword against his own son. "It seems / All one, it seems all one. There's no distinction. / Which is my son?"

In Cymen's absence, taken out to rest by his despairing

wife, Hoel and Martina, Cymen's daughter, are drawn into a Romeo-and-Juliet love affair by sympathy and misery. Martina is enchanted by his sincerity, helplessness, and bravery. Like so many of the women Fry is to cast in minor comic roles, Alizon Eliot in *The Lady*, Rosabel in *Venus Observed*, and Gelda in *The Dark*, she begins to love blindly, passionately, and sentimentally. Yet she is as unaware of the true state of her emotions as Hoel is of his.

To extend his theme, although the stasis at the center of the play is thereby only partly concealed, Fry introduces the most appealing character in the play, Merlin who with his foresight, benevolence, and mythic fancy is a choral embodiment of the Jungian collective unconscious. Although he has mellowed into a pacific presider over endurance and forgiveness, he still recalls his origins as the Arthurian exhorter to knightly violence.

Merlin's lofty, enlightened mysticism is balanced by the lively earthiness of Colgrin, Cymen's lazy, good-natured steward. Merlin develops the play's theme lyrically while Colgrin's sloth, cowardice, and irreverent wit mock the life-destroying piety of the suppliant wives, the self-inflated boastfulness of the warriors, and the puritanical idolatry of discipline to cover sordid lusts and greed in an entire society. "The best life is led horizontal / And absolutely unconscious." He is the typical parasite with roots going back to Plautine comedy.

As the simmering conflict between Cymen and his family over Hoel revives and begins to boil over, it is again interrupted, this time by an alarm of danger. Wolves are attacking the family's sheep, a dramatic metaphor of the symbolic Christian community menaced by forces of evil and irrationality. The men rush out, joined by Hoel, the crisis bringing a temporary end to the artificial barriers between the Jutes and their captive. Meanwhile, Merlin glimpses a new dispensation as Roman emissaries approach the British shore. "A ship in full foliage rides in / Over the February foam, and rests / Upon Britain." Hoel's heroism against the wolves is perversely misinterpreted by the brothers as another attack on their gods, and they at last persuade Cymen to take action. But to their horror, he slanders the gods, renounces sacrifice, and finally tears down the altar, challenging the gods to "Come down and silence me! / Then at least I shall have some kind of part / With all the rest." His closeness to Hoel has become even more marked, for like the captive he too has lost an acceptable identity, a persona and a name, with a sense of cosmic loneliness. "Is separation between man and Gods / So complete? Can't you even bring me to silence?" he asks.

In the thick of his confusion, Cymen is summoned to meet Augustine, to hear the message from Christian Rome. In his absence Martina and Hoel cement their growing passion as the spiteful, intriguing relatives eavesdrop, a recurring device with Fry. Their vitality overcomes the artificial barriers of clan and race as they exchange confidences. "What simple-witted things the affections are, / That can't perceive whether people are enemies or friends." Martina's innocent kiss is perverted by the conspiring watchers to a kiss of death, love giving rise to blood lust. They kill Hoel—tying him to a tree, his arms spread to form a cross, and stabbing him with a spear. Hoel is a martyr in spite of himself, however, for he wants to live. Like all of Fry's enlightened characters he knows that nothing living can be evil. A violent death can only poison the earth from which all life springs. In Cymen's words, "The blood flows, the ground soaks it up, / The poisoned nightshade grows, the fears go on." Violence flows back against its doer in a movement of nemesis unless the original sin is exorcised by grace.

Cymen returns with the newly-proclaimed Christianity, only to discover Hoel's crucifixion and use it, a little precipitously, for a sermon.

> We are afraid
> To live by rule of God, which is forgiveness,
> Mercy, and compassion, fearing that by these
> We shall be ended. And yet if we could bear
> These three through dread and terror and terror's doubt,
> Daring to return good for evil without thought

Of what will come, I cannot think
We should be the losers. Do we believe
There is no strength in good or power in God?
God give us courage to exist in God,
And lonely flesh be welcome to creation.

Although Hoel's sacrifice has resulted from blind anger
and could never be sufficiently condemned, God's willingness to forgive even so heinous a crime as murder has been
proved in the sacrifice "by God / To God in the body of
God with man." The fear and animalistic cruelty of the
brothers has been subsumed first by Cymen's doubt, then
his growing compassion and finally by a transcendent
Christian forgiveness. Even the churlish and superstitious
fanatics, the brothers, finally emerge as misled rather than
vicious, the inheritors of a new dispensation.

Thor breaks no new ground stylistically, but exploits the
audacious plays on words, inversions and reversed expectations so typical of Fry's work so far. Within the predominantly blank verse framework, Fry manages to encompass
wisecracks along with oracular visions, double-entendre
with rapid-fire line-bouncing. Colgrin has some of the best
jokes, looking for a sword he never intends to use one
moment: "I've got you on my weapon's point. / (Where
the Valhalla is it?)," and being brought up short at another, when his wife says: "And *this* isn't going to get the
baby washed." COLGRIN: "*What* baby washed?" Ridicule
of the pagan superstitions generally comes across more
effectively than veneration of the half-remembered Trin-
ity, as when Hoel recalls, "I was only / Allowed to have
one, though in that One, they said, / There were three."
Fry is much more vivid and surprising in the long inter-
ludes of Merlin, however much they halt the action, when
he fully exploits the pathetic fallacy.

> *old Joseph's faithful staff*
> *Breaking into scarlet bud in the falling snow.*
> *But, as I said at the time, the miracle*
> *Was commonplace: staves of chestnut wood*
> *And maywood and the like perform it every year.*

The family's paganism is decisively pinpricked with a number of deft slashes: "It isn't / Easy to keep on the windy side of Woden / As anyone knows" or "we swing back on time, and hope the gods / Forget the indecision."

Throughout, however, alliteration is prominent—"silver skulked / Waiting for skill," Orwellian negatives appear—"Do the undeed," and repetitions are used, "Quest and conquest and quest again." Strong emotion tends to emerge in a rigid and exact, but rare pentametric line: "I curse this kingdom, water, rock and soil!" Characteristically, the longest speeches in the play are invocations, such as those by Merlin, by Cymen before the altar, and the reports of miracles by messengers.

Thor is not Fry's most ambitious play nor his most effective. An examination of its defects lends some support to Arrowsmith's contention that Fry's plays are padded one-acts. One of its weaknesses is the failure to dramatize the incredible miracles; another is the coercion of the action, or even its replacement, by language; the play has no middle, only a beginning and an end loosely connected. Then too, Cymen's role in initiating and finally resolving the central conflict far outweighs his actual contribution to the action, while Hoel's sensitive, confused gropings seem out of character with the herculean feats in which he is reported to have engaged offstage. For all the play's flaws, however, Cymen's inner struggle is vigorous and credible, while Martina's growing affection for Hoel is handled with a tactful, delicate subtlety. While Fry uses a large stock of British mythico-historical material, the theme of the play appears fully contemporary.

7

Venus Observed

Venus Observed[1] was first produced on January 18, 1950, at the St. James, London. Sir Lawrence Olivier, who had commissioned it, played the lead. It was a month in which Fry reached the zenith of his theatrical renown. *The Lady* was just concluding its run, the Company of Four revived *The Boy* on January 19, and within another week, Fry's translation of Anouilh's *Ring Round the Moon* (*L'Invitation au Chateau*) opened at the Globe.

Venus Observed was planned, Fry has told us,

> as one of a series of four comedies, a comedy for each of the seasons of the year, four comedies of mood. . . . In *Venus* the season is autumn, the scene is a house beginning to fall into decay, the characters, most of them, are in middle life.[2]

The eclipse of the sun, the Halloween scenes, and above all, the Duke, with his declining vigor, fear of death, and decision to remarry complete the autumnal mood. Not only the Duke, but nature and civilization are in decay.

Fry's second full-length comedy grows from his earlier practice within the tragicomic tradition. Once again as in *A Phoenix* and *The Lady*, a double triangle appears, entangling the Duke and his son Edgar in competition for Perpetua while Perpetua and one of the Duke's former mistresses try to enlighten Altair. The play is designed characteristically not to attack sin and evil, but to ridicule a lack of self-knowledge. Fry reuses the more conventional pattern of comedy by giving the Duke a hypothetical

competitor who is one of the mistress' husbands, a traditional offstage buffoon who sustains "a level depth / Of
dullness." However, the Duke is a transitional figure, an
inverted Mendip. Both he and Thomas know life is both
miraculous and contemptible, but Mendip rebels by attempting suicide while the Duke's rejection consists of a
lunge at ideality. As a blocking force the Duke is unusually effective for comedy, for while Virilius was cleverly
manipulated in A *Phoenix* and Tyson and Humphrey
evaded (though with some difficulty) in *The Lady*, the
Duke delays the consummation of Edgar's and Perpetua's
love, even at the end of the play. He looks ahead to the
Countess in this respect; for all her virtues Rosmarin
renders Gettner impotent. Perpetua is another of Fry's
abundant, independent daughters of the Life Force. She is
the girlish type like Dynamene and Jennet, refined by
civilization, yet passionately opposed to sham and vulgar-
ity.

Yet if Fry was to work again with the comic patterns,
conventions and types he had already learned to wield so
brilliantly, he faced unique problems too. He needed to
avoid self-imitation, opening at the same time a new
approach to the traditional devices. Most importantly, if
the Duke were to remain both an active and likable competitor he must obstruct his young rival but not irration-
ally; he must be witty, passionate, and even cynical, but a
figure with whom an audience could readily sympathise.
And in the course of the play, Fry must deepen its import
and extend its implications with symbolism, both Christian and pagan, in a fresh and original way.

The title of the play puns on both the goddess and the
planet, promiscuous sexual satiety and intellectual isolation. The Duke's onetime philanderings have been followed, now that he is middle-aged, by lonely stargazing.
Nor should the title's echo of Otway's *Venice Preserved*
be overlooked, for in both plays a young woman faces an
agonizing choice between conflicting loyalties. Moreover,
Otway's subtitle, "A Plot Discovered," fits both plays.
Conspiracies, the reuniting of long-separated father and
daughter, imprisonment of the daughter, an unsuccessful

attempt at seduction, self-destructive acts, and the theme of forgiveness occur in both.

Venus begins with an apparent absurdity: the Duke of Altair (altitude + air) has invited three of his former mistresses to visit his estate in order that his son Edgar may perform the judgment of Paris. Ironically he seeks matrimony as a refuge from "the parcelling out of heaven in small beauties," which he has enjoyed promiscuously, and uses an eclipse for an ostensible reunion. Hilda Taylor-Snell is Aphrodite and Jessie Dill is Athena; Rosabel, his eventual choice, is Hera, perhaps accounting for the Duke's name "Hereward." Hilda is gently ironic and imperturbable, and Jessie is a sort of middle-aged Doto, now charitable, serenely jolly, and tolerant. Rosabel is a sensitive and impressionable, failed actress, the only one of the three touched deeply by the Duke's love. But surrounding their earthly palpability is an aura of symbolic association for they are not only goddesses, as Fry suggests, but also Furies, mother-wife-and-daughter figures, and the Fates (mentioned in A Phoenix): Clotho (spins), Lachesis (twists) and Atropos (severs). Fry has invoked the choice among three love-objects which has occurred not only in classical myth, but in religion, fairy tale, and literature. Shakespeare uses it at least twice, in the suitors' choice among the three caskets in The Merchant of Venice and in Lear's choice among his three daughters. In his analysis of the archetype Freud points out that although the third of the goddesses is Death itself, in the judgment of Paris she is the Goddess of Love, motifs Fry has intertwined throughout his drama. Where the Duke tries to exercise choice, in reality he obeys compulsion as he implicitly admits to Edgar: "Equality is a mortuary word. Just choose." Choice stands in the place of necessity, of destiny. And that which he chooses is not, he hopes, a thing of horror—either death in the flames or, in forcing Perpetua, a self-concept of lustful tyrant, but mythic rejuvenation through love. Most of the play's classical allusions to the apples of Melanion, the pursuit of Actaeon by Artemis, the rise of Venus from the sea, and the ever-youthful Endymion symbolize the rebirth of nature, the rise of the phoenix, as the eclipse of the sun by the moon suggests.

The action centering around the Duke has, as Jacob Adler points out, many parallels in Shakespeare, particularly *The Tempest*. Like Prospero, Altair is a Duke trying to arrange other people's lives, his tower, telescope, and mirror providing him with an esoteric quality resembling Prospero's magic. Both men are aware of double-crossing, discover the futility of permanent withdrawal from the world, and finally resign their power to youth. Yet even closer parallels can be found in Shaw, particularly *Caesar and Cleopatra* or his Chekhovian *Heartbreak House* (a good subtitle for *Venus*, incidentally). Shotover is also an old man matched with a young woman, surrounded by middle-aged people in an autumnal era, his weapon-making serving as a kind of equivalent for the Duke's "magic." Moreover, the Faustian motif, the triad of "goddesses," the comic burglar, and the bombing raid (like the fire) are paralleled in Fry. And Perpetua's spectacular entrance may owe something to the crash of Shaw's Lina Szczepanowska through the greenhouse roof in the first act of *Misalliance*. As for the eclipse, Fry was perfectly capable of inventing it, but two had occurred just before he wrote the play, one on July 9, 1945 and another on May 20, 1947. Although neither was visible in England, both were widely reported in the press.

Once Perpetua arrives, however, Edgar insists on performing the judgment of Paris for himself, and Rosabel attacks the Duke for his cynical disregard for human feelings:

> How can you tell who loves, or when or why they love,
> You without a single beat of heart
> Worth measuring? You sit up here all night
> Looking at the stars, travelling farther and farther
> Away from living people. I hate your telescope!

[which is both phallic symbol and an emblem of the Duke's detachment]. Refusing to recognize the Duke's tolerant geniality as a virtue, she insists on a permanent, unchanging affection. But the Duke has learned that man shrinks when seen from a cosmic perspective, although Life compensates. "To take us separately is to stare / At mud; only together, at long range, / We coalesce in light." The Duke has known and forgiven the thieving of his agent Reedbeck, a delightfully unprincipled man of exquisite sensibility. But unknown to him, Dominic has also discovered his father's duplicity and, like Rosabel, demands an absolute—in Dominic's case, moral perfection. Ironically the Duke and Reedbeck find themselves in oddly parallel circumstances, although their names symbolize the higher and lower vices, unfeeling intellectuality, and covert thievery or "Reed-bequity." While both of them try to reunite divided families, their ends are frustrated by their sons who reveal, one openly and the other conspiratorially, oedipal rebellions.

Perpetua's dramatic appearance captivates the Duke, but she soon admits that she has just been released from prison in America. She had been sent there because,

> I was thought to be unsafe
> For democracy, because I broke, or shot,
> Or burnt, a good many things, or rather—and this
> Is the reason—a bad many things: the unsightly,
> The gimcrack, the tedious, the hideous, the spurious,
> The harmful.

When Edgar and the Duke begin to quarrel openly over her, she whips out a tiny pistol and shatters the apple the Duke is prepared to offer, reasserting her rebellious idealism. She is still dedicated to the destruction of the ugly and harmful. "It appeared to be, in a misty way, / Like a threat to my new-come freedom." Her William Tell gesture may stem from Milton, via Thomas Mendip in *The Lady*, who had described Adam as

> shot
> To bits with the core of an apple
> Which some fool of a serpent in the artillery
> Had shoved into God's cannon (The Lady, 26).

An Americanized daughter of a deserting mother, Perpet-ua has returned her revolutionary ideals—after America has ironically repudiated them—to the seat of supposedly enlightened aristocracy. Her act also spurs Rosabel into covert, but potentially more destructive rebellion with another kind of firearm.

Inconsistencies in the Duke's character, the fantastic array of symbols and hand props, as well as the echoes from "sources"—including Fry's other work and his read-ing—add to the play's air of improvisation. Fry has claimed,

> As for the method of writing: I certainly seldom, if ever, start on a play until I have seen its whole shape and conclusion. I don't think I always know precisely why I have chosen that "story" until I am working.[3]

For all his previous plays, Fry's comment can stand. But as Peter Brook has recounted, Fry began Venus without having "seen its whole shape and conclusion," an unusual procedure for him. After finishing the first act (late in the summer of 1948),

> Fry got stuck. He discovered he didn't know what hap-pened next. . . . An observatory. An eclipse. And then what happens? I don't know. Perhaps something in a decay-ing temple by a lake.[4]

So Fry dropped the incomplete play and translated An-ouilh's L'Invitation au Chateau for Brook. In the process, however, he must have read or been reminded of a brief passage of dialogue in Anouilh's Madame Colombe which solved his plot difficulties in Venus. All the essential ac-tion is there in a brief speech, some of which he may have inserted in the first act later: the pistol shot, the fire, one competitor's "eclipse" by another, the passionate embrace and the last-minute rescue.

POETE-CHERI   Was it not at about the same time that Boni Despinglettes set fire to his hotel for you, Madame Alexandra?

MADAME ALEXANDRA How crazy! I had been stall-
ing him for a year. We were having dinner at his home,
with friends. The conversation was revolving around
Neron. I mentioned my admiration for this so astonishing
being who had understood life so beautifully. I said of
that gypsy, I probably would have liked him. Despinglettes went pale, rose, took a candelabra and without say-
ing a word, set fire to the drapes. The servants wanted to
rush in with water jugs. But he drew his gun from his
pocket and threatened to shoot them if they made a move.
We were all standing up, all of us pale, watching the
drapes burn. When the flames reached the ceiling, I went
to him without a word and I kissed him on the mouth.
The servants took the opportunity to throw water on the
fire. That is how we saved the building.[5]

With some adjustments to the first act, the brief passage from Anouilh may have supplied Fry with his compli-
cation, crisis and resolution—although other sources, from
Fry's own practice and reading, meld with the *Madame
Colombe* elements. The Ophelia-role which Rosabel had
once played prepares for another parallel in the action.
Perpetua will fail as dutiful daughter (Ophelia to Polonius) even as Rosabel will slip as lover (Ophelia to Hamlet). And in the act to follow, Edgar will move too soon,
too impetuously—in shooting his father as Hamlet killed
Polonius—while the Duke, perilously like Polonius, will
delay almost too long in withdrawing from the burning
tower.

Ironically Perpetua and the Duke have similar personality cores or essences: both are passionate, idealistic, and
impetuous by nature. The Duke's despair at ever attaining
his ideal love emerges in promiscuity, while Perpetua—
another frustrated idealist—has been an anarchist. They
are both people of instinct, for whom rebellion and self-
destruction are far more natural than conformity. Balance
and reconciliation, which both of them seem to have
achieved at the beginning of the play, have resulted more
from frustration than rational deliberation. While their
vitality, spontaneity, and witty inventiveness are what

make them so attractive as characters, it is precisely Fry's success in gaining our belief in these qualities which makes their final acceptance of chastened conformity in the third act appear so unmotivated and inconsistent.

The first scene in Act II is set near the now-disused Temple of the Ancient Virtues, an oblique glance at civilization's morally decrepit situation. Rosabel's pyromania, the disaffected mistresses' encouragement of Edgar's discontent, and Perpetua's imminent waste in atonement for Reedbeck's sins suggest that a whole society is breaking up. Although the Duke has regained the initiative, his arbitrary summoning of the mistresses, his humiliation of both Edgar and Rosabel, and finally his assertion of his "right" to Perpetua cast him in the role of oppressor—despite his urbane likability—who deserves to be defeated. Moreover, the battle between the "ins" and the "outs" grows out of the alternation of scenes between the decrepit observatory filled with the newest scientific equipment and the verdant Temple from which so many duchesses had announced so many pregnancies.

First Dominic and then Edgar face similar dilemmas. Having discovered his father's indiscretions, Dominic rather melodramatically forces his agreement to the marriage of Perpetua to the Duke. Reedbeck is a high-minded, but dishonest version of the chaplain in *The Lady*. He has justified his covert larceny by the superiority of his sense of beauty over the Duke's, a social version of Rosabel's argument: "I care so much for civilization, / Its patrician charm, its grave nobility; / He cares so little." Thus Perpetua's rebellious idealism and Dominic's guilty moralizing are the two halves of their father's character.

Edgar has moved through the same sequence of roles played by Dominic, first as overprotected son (just awaking from his boyhood dream of riding and horses), then as anti-authoritarian, and finally as a chastened but partly victorious symbol of the "new order." While the Duke and Perpetua play at archery, they arrange to meet that night in the observatory. In the garden Edgar broods over his new rivalry with his father, torn with jealousy, insufficiency, and anger. In the struggle he is abetted first by Hilda: "it's greatly important / There *should* be room for both of you." Like Perpetua he hunts the hunter, watches the watcher. Edgar's near-castration of his father with a cupidic arrow extends an oedipal situation into a social revolution. But Perpetua spurns Edgar under duress, and her lie about retiring early misleads Rosabel, who decides: "I shall send his observatory / Where Nero's Rome has gone. / I'll blaze a trail / That he can follow towards humanity!"

The ensuing action, placed in the Duke's observatory room, is the longest uninterrupted scene in the play. As in most games, both the Duke and Perpetua pretend to be completely candid, while ironically withholding from one another a secret known to both: Reedbeck's thievery. The Duke explains to Perpetua that he is not a lustful sensualist, but a deep and sensitive thinker who has undergone "man's ordeal by star." In his brief marriage he had only glimpsed "the one twin-hearted permanence," and he had experienced nothing beyond the sudden flush of passion. With her death at Edgar's birth, "one life put the other out," and he wonders about his philandering: had it stemmed from "making do because the best / Was done?" Or was he trying to "find the face which, willingly, / I should never let pass?", a quest for the missing platonic half?

The Duke playfully suggests a magical test appropriate to *All Hallows' Eve*. An ancient mirror, he tells her,

> *Is so potent it can draw the future*
> *Into the glass, and show shadows of husbands*
> *To girls who sit and comb their hair.*

Again he offers her an apple, drawing together in a symbolic unity the apples of Paris, of Eden, of Halloween and Atalanta. In its edenic aspect, it points up the pathos of the Temple of Ancient Virtues, the decaying eden of his spirit which the Duke hopes to restore. It also works back from "Perpetua Perpetual" to Venus (as goddess), to the star as seen through the Duke's telescope, to the Christian

Lucifer, and so to Eden again. But it is all done by "mirrors," a reflection of both characters' disguised motives. Like Saturn, whose image once glinted from Ariadne's mirror, the Duke hopes that he himself will appear as if by magic in the crystal held by Perpetua. Yet his illusion is abruptly destroyed. Perpetua says, "It seemed to be Edgar," and their undisguised hostility tears the mask off their pretenses as Altair admits that he had forgiven Reedbeck's thefts from him in writing.

PERPETUA   How happy do you feel to know you tried
    For a bride by this conspiracy of silence?
DUKE   How happy do you feel to know you were ready
    To take a husband to make that silence absolute?

Yet when the crackling of Rosabel's fire interrupts them, apparently cutting off their escape, the Duke and Perpetua turn to one another. In the face of disaster the Duke is calm, even stoical. Seeing in their *Liebestod* a perfect "union / Of beauty born and beauty reft away," he pleads for Perpetua's love. For her part she is startled into an embrace which the Duke misinterprets as passion.

> And I, *pursuing love, no farther than this*
> *Pure outcry of recognition,*
> *Possess it most faithfully.*

Yet Perpetua's kiss, like that of Gelda to Gettner in *The Dark* is not love, but the affirmation of human solidarity in misery. The Duke's desire for love is both aggravated and assimilated by imminent annihilation.

In the nick of time a mock *deus ex machina* appears. Reddleman and Bates arrive in the guise of classical divinities. Reddleman, the cowardly lion-tamer, has gained his nerve again, while the burgling Bates has at last discovered a rationale for his old ladder-climbing mania. Ironically, their arrival suggests that rescuing victims from a fire is like saving free will from passion, although none of the farcical exuberance is sacrificed. Bates helps Perpetua down a ladder, while Reddleman and the Duke brave the fiery stairs.

Although Anouilh's *Madame Colombe* must have given

Fry his spectacular climax, the repeated use of fires in his plays suggests that the passage had more than a chance appeal. Real or symbolic fires appear in all his plays but *The Firstborn* and *The Dark is Light Enough*. A key moment in his unpublished *The Tower* (1939) is the fire which destroyed Tewkesbury Abbey in 1178. In both *The Boy* and *Thor, with Angels*, the crucifixions have fiery elements and three of the soldiers in *A Sleep of Prisoners* undergo purgation by flame like Shadrac, Meshac, and Obednego (whom Fry mentions in *Venus*). The phoenix is a key symbol in his first comedy and Humphrey in *The Lady*, Rosabel in *Venus* and Henry II in *Curtmantle* are all at a critical time in their lives revealed as pyromaniac. Their illness is defined by the *Psychiatric Dictionary* as "Sexual excitement aroused by the sight of conflagrations." The definition continues that often "incendiaries set fire to their beds, as though to indicate the still active enuristic source of their pyromanic character trait." [6] Significantly, just as the phoenix sets its nest afire, Rosabel ignites the bed which she had once shared with the Duke in the observatory and Henry II ignites the town which is his birthplace.

The third act is a Saturnalia of confessions and reconciliations, bringing together initially the play's two sadomasochists, Rosabel and Dominic. With her aggressive, destructive urges drained off, Rosabel pleads for punishment. The equally guilt-ridden Dominic obliges, only to learn finally that he has erred in thinking more of the sin than of the sinner.

His observatory reduced to ashes although his life is saved, the Duke now understands an existential truth. Saddened by his new insight into life's imperfections, he regrets his consciousness which only estranges him from nature. Yet by recognizing the unavoidable isolation of men from each other, the Duke understands the shortcomings men have in common.

I forgive even
The unrevealing revelation of love

That lifts a lid purely
To close it, and leaves us knowing that greater things
Are close, but not to be disclosed
Though we die for them.

On the basis of his recognition of human shortcomings, he accepts Rosabel as his marriage partner.

In this way Dominic and the Duke polarize the moral balance of the play. In contrast to Dominic's moral literalism, the Duke's indulgence of human frailty led him not only to condone Reedbeck's thefts, but to hire Bates in spite of his burgling, and Reddleman despite his cowardice. Thus Dominic and the Duke embody the contrast between divine and human justice, illustrating the superiority of Christian love which supersedes the law.

The ironies in V*enus* are neat and symmetrical. Perpetua's moral passion sexually exhilarates the Duke, bringing about the rebirth of his quest for lost youth, while the Duke's love forces Perpetua to abandon her entrapment of him to save her father. Perpetua's admission that her love for him was of the moment so impresses him that the Duke forgives her, while the lesson of the Duke's lofty forbearance moderates any rush into an illicit affair with Edgar. The Duke will expand into a husband while Perpetua dwindles into a wife.

As Fry points out, the theme of the play is loneliness, and the Duke "accepts, at last, that a man's completion is not in his life time or in his flesh but in some distance in time, or not in time at all." [7] Just as the sun re-emerging from its eclipse by the moon presages the rebirth of nature, so the purification of the Duke's affections may prophesy hope for civilization in its ordeal.

Fry's language in V*enus* is more artificial, glittering and exuberant than in any of his other plays. The Joycean puns ("corruscating on thin ice"), the Shavian "Reedbequity," and the Audenic assonance ("foment of wild flamboyant rose") are as prominent as ever. But despite an occasional misfire or bad joke, like Perpetua's "To please, I always aim"—it is not inappropriate or merely decorative. Like his theme and characters it has the freshness of improvisation, the cleverness of audacious humor and the self-mockery of fantastic whimsy. "My original / Syntax, like original sin, grows vastier / In the dark," says the Duke. Or it may convey the lushness of the things it describes, endowing inanimate objects with human qualities.

> *I will offer her*
> *The cloudy peach, the bristling pineapple,*
> *The dropsical pear, the sportive orange,*
> *Apricot, sloe, King William, or a carillon*
> *Of grapes, but not, as God's my judge, an apple.*

Edgar's list is not a mere catalog, but a vivid, concrete expression of the essence both of the fruits he lists and of varied personality types. He also subtly reminds his father that people may be too varied to be easily manipulated, that ("as God's my judge") he plans to act according to his own nature rather than as his father arbitrarily assumes he should.

Fry is even less obliged than usual to approximate everyday speech. His characters are unusually sophisticated, sensitive and histrionic. Besides this, the play's issues have no relevance at all to social utility, problems like slum housing, prostitution or drug addiction, which must dictate the tone and diction of prose realism. Fry is more concerned with the inexorable decay of the physical senses, forgiveness, the mystery of existence, and the irrational riddle of being. For these "problems" he is forced to seek an idiom and dramatic analogies which, strictly speaking, reveal the essences or "whatness" of perceptions not related to the appearance of things in time and space at all.

As a result the careful imitation of flat, commonplace speech accents, and the logical progression of ideas are largely abandoned. In their place appears a heightened, associative rhetoric of self-revelation and sensation. His comic, unlettered servants, it is true, have stock comic accents.

> *There are faces*
> *As can be mauled about wiv, and there are faces*
> *As can't be mauled about wiv. Mine can't*
> *Be mauled about wiv.*

But the characters can be distinguished by other means, particularly by the careful auditor. The peppery, sly Reedbeck breaks into song one moment, falls into elaborate circumlocution at another ("the east wind, smoking fires, / Revolution, debility"), or snaps out a string of epithets: "You spigoted, bigoted, operculated prig!," but the range and intensity of his emotions are accurately reflected at each changing moment. The mistresses are carefully differentiated in their speech rhythms and diction, while Perpetua entices the Duke as much through the unpredictability, energy, and winsomeness of her speech as through her youth and beauty. Her long (44-line) single-sentence speech to the Duke has been both admired and attacked as a tour de force:

> *There isn't any reason*
> *Why a sentence, I suppose, once it begins . . .*
> *. . . shouldn't go*
> *Endlessly moving in grave periphrasis*
> *And phrase in linking phrase. . . .*

But she is relieving her own sense of tension, guilt, and uncertainty which intensify, through her delay, both her own qualms and the Duke's passion. Fry's language, then, is an extension of the theme and mood of the play, parodying and cleverly mocking the pretensions and seriousness of modern verse.

Although *Venus Observed* has been highly, even extravagantly praised, it is not hard to see why it is not his best play. The Duke shifts course so often with so little preparation that his character seems to be inconsistent. With the benefit of hindsight we may decide it is not: he still has too much vitality, too much impatience with approaching death to allow his careful, if zany plan to deter a sudden infatuation with Perpetua. Yet his final choice of Rosabel for his wife and his future relationship to Edgar—to mention only a couple of difficulties—seem un-worldly to the point of irrationality. His very complexity, humaneness, and tolerance overbalance the play. The Duke's virtues so far outweigh his excesses that no significant change in his character could possibly be convincing. As a result, most ot the other characters have little to do, aside from providing opportunities for the Duke's traits to reveal themselves. Hilda and Jessie, likable as they are, seem distractingly in the way after the first scene; Rosabel's actions verge so perilously on the psychopathic that her sudden penitence looks suspiciously like neurosis; and Edgar practically disappears after the first act. The play is nearly over by the end of the second act. As a result the third act is little more than a series of soliloquies. Finally, while the plethora of hand props such as the apple and pistol, bow and quiver, telescope and bed, mirror and lamp release a rich over-layer of witty and mythic associations, they tend to slow or coerce the action.

Despite Fry's difficulties with proportion in the play, the character of the Duke is a high-level achievement. Altair renounces the greater for the lesser blessing, revealing in the process an admirable combination of endurance, insight, good humor, and forgiveness. As in *The Lady* the Duke and Perpetua represent opposing views of life, both of which are mitigated by disaster. Perpetua receives from the Duke a clear sense of mystery, while he derives from her a heightened awareness of life's impossibilities.

8

A Sleep of Prisoners

A *Sleep of Prisoners* [1] is probably Fry's best religious play, using an experimental form to present orthodox ideas. The play reaffirms Fry's faith that man can grasp hope through an endurance of suffering: "the play could not end in a glorious suffering, or even the indication of victory—we have too far to travel for that—but certainly, in hope," [2] he told the *New York Times* (the source for other comment in the chapter). While Fry was thinking about two other plays in the summer of 1950 (probably *The Dark is Light Enough* and *Curtmantle*), his friends Martin Browne and Michael MacOwan asked him, on behalf of the Religious Drama Society, to write a play for the Festival of Britain. Fry recalled that three miles from his cottage in the Cotswolds in the village church of Burford, six Cromwellian soldiers had been imprisoned. One of them had even carved his name on the font— "Antony Sedley Prisner 1649." So the germ of *A Sleep* was sown. It was to be "a play about a church turned into a prison camp, the prisoners being not Cromwellians, but men of our own time."

It is tempting to read the play as a sequel to Sean O'Casey's *The Plough and the Stars*, where four of the characters are taken off to be imprisoned in a Protestant church after the Irish Rebellion has been crushed. The design of the play, Fry decided as he discussed it with Browne, would be to show a group of men—four rather than six—as they seemed on the surface to each other. Then they would sleep and dream, each man dreaming of the other three and of himself, so that each character is seen four times over. Their dreams are conditioned by their prison, the episodes resembling a series of four biblical parables.

The play was successfully performed on May 15, 1951, at St. Thomas' Church, Regent Street, London, and for the first time in America, at St. James' Church, New York City, on October 16, 1951. It was then taken on extensive tours in England, the United States, and on the Continent. But in Australia the play ran into trouble. After a single performance in Sidney, on February 1, 1952, not only the play itself but the entire series which it was intended to initiate was banned by the Episcopal hierarchy. Despite the high appreciation with which the audience greeted the play, both the Archbishop and the Bishop Coadjutor of Sydney reaffirmed their ban: a church was no place for a dramatic performance.

The ban imposed by the Australian churchmen is a reminder of the uneasy and often hostile jockeying for influence which has always disturbed church-theater relations. Any objective observer can find in *A Sleep*, as in all the medieval Mystery plays, an element of near-blasphemy. God himself is impersonated rather humorously, there are several onstage murders, and Holy Writ is occasionally inverted, even burlesqued. "I said Let there be love, / And there wasn't enough light, you say?" And again, "You know what Absalom / Said to the tree? 'You're getting in my hair'." Since military language is used throughout, by common, uneducated soldiers, their idiom is occasionally coarse and profane. "What the hell do you think we're stuck here for / Locked in like lunatics?" Yet the language of the Mysteries is often more vulgar, and the situations even more farcical. Fry is banking heavily on the sanity of his audience, their ability to see the constant elements of faith underlying the unwise, even grotesque antics of fallible mankind.

While the play has roots both in the Bible and in the medieval Mysteries (although the technical debt is small), it also assimilates techniques from expressionism, theatricalism, and existentialism. Like the expressionists Fry has, first of all, reduced his characters to types whose names recall biblical precursors: David King, Peter Able, Tim Meadows, and Joe Adams. Their names are no more precise than the general terms often used by the expressionists, such as Father, Son, Body, or Soul. Secondly, the action in A *Sleep* unfolds in a succession of scenes, denoting stages of the characters' development towards a spiritual goal. Each of the episodes describes a journey, with Adam stopping on his way out of Paradise, Absalom trying to evade the avenging Joab, Abraham taking Isaac up a mountain for sacrifice, and finally, three of the soldiers trudging through a furnace like Shadrac, Meshac, and Obednego. Thirdly, there is no protagonist or antagonist as such. All of the characters are projections of Mankind's inner struggle. "I wanted to move from division to unity," Fry has commented. In each of the dreams the action unfolds on a purely fantastic plane where the laws of causality are suspended, and the logic of dream prevails. Hence the characters tend to split, double, and multiply.

Like the expressionists and Pirandello, whom they influenced, Fry has assimilated Ibsen's realism, Strindberg's psychology, and Bergson's philosophy. With Pirandello he has seen that man in life represents a variety of roles, including the role of himself as he sees himself and the roles that his fellow men thrust upon him. Existentialism can also be detected in the play, for each character perceives that life is absurd, filling him with nausea, dread, and anguish. Each is trapped by the concept formed of him by another character.

> O God, are we
> To be shut up here in what other men do
> And watch ourselves be ground and battered
> Into their sins?

Their hell is other people, not so much existential fires and torments. "What they like to call us / Matters more than anything at heart." What each character has lost—and must find again—is a publicly acceptable identity and name. Their captivity by dreams, by dark phantasms of Original Sin, duplicates on the unconscious level their soul's imprisonment in the church (symbolizing the body). "A dream / Has got you prisoner, Davey, like / The world has got us all." As each man is forced to undergo his *tour abolie*, his search for origins, each discovers that he has lost free will. They dream the nightmare that the possibility of life is no longer open to them: "Who are we, Dave, who / Are we? . . . the open air /Feels like a barrack square." Yet the characters in the play are also comic to a degree. Each one has a fixed personality trait—aggressiveness or lack of it, reasonableness or a reliance on the rules — which he repeats in a machine-like way, trapped as Fry says by "facades behind which we hide our spirits."

But the play never dissolves completely into a psychic fantasy. Fry wanted both the technical freedom which expressionism and theatricalism could give him and the hold on individuality and colloquial, down-to-earth speech of concrete realism. It is in the humane attributes of character that *A Sleep* differs from the plays of the expressionists. Retrospection, reverie, and psychological confusion play their part, but Fry never fails to bring his characters back to reality. They are people, and not mere abstractions. Bergson's *élan vital* is visible here. Man is forever aware of his limitations and inadequacies; nevertheless, he is driven to express his uniqueness and identity against those forces which would reduce him to a machine or worse, to nothingness. Thus Fry is less abstract in his characterization, less incoherent in his presentation of scenes than the expressionists.

Secondly, Fry's commentator (Meadows) and the play-within-a-play technique no longer indicate, as they once would have, a direct line to Pirandello. He is too independent, too imaginative to be enslaved by another man's system. He certainly invokes a sense of metaphysical anguish which appears in Pirandello and later in Anouilh, who owes a debt to the great Italian. But their versions of erotic relations *in extremis* are totally absent from *A Sleep*. When they do appear in Fry, they are treated not

as material for tragedy but as Molieresque humours. Infecting such characters as Humphrey in *The Lady* and
Rosabel in *Venus*, the sexual passions must be purged, to
further social health and stability, or placed in romantic
juxtaposition with death, a *Liebesod*.

Finally, although the theme of suffering recurs throughout *A Sleep*, Fry makes much less of dread and death than
he does of man's self-centeredness, vanity, and rigidity. It
is not the sombre and depressed moods he stresses most,
but the way in which after pain and anguish the characters "unmortify themselves: to affirm life and assimilate
death and persevere in joy," as he has written in "Comedy." Joy and exultation constantly appear in the play, not
only at the end, but in the impassioned language, the
recurring spirit of relief and optimism. "God dips his hand
in death to wash the wound, / Takes evil to inoculate our
lives / Against infectious evil."

The play begins in the evening, enacts a series of conflicts during the night, and arrives at a synthesis of unity
and new hope as morning dawns. The pattern of each
episode embodies the shape of the play as a whole, moving
through purpose to passion and then to perception. Four
soldiers have been locked in a church by "Towsers" (an
imaginary nickname for the enemy). Private Peter Able is
so incapable of anger and hate that he clashes almost
immediately with Private David King, a man of action.
King fights evil with such dedication that Peter's needling
good nature finally drives him to try to strangle his partner. In their conflict, Peter is the questioner. Seeing man's
alienation from nature, he can visualize only one remedy:
not more evil but good. "The world blows up, there's
Peter there in the festering / Bomb-hole making cups of
tea." In David's world, however, crime is met by crime.
He resents evil so quickly that he partakes of it. He
doesn't like to fight but feels he must. "We're at war with
them, aren't we? And if we are / They're no blaming use!"
Cruder perhaps, like Rosmarin's friends in *The Dark*, he is
careful to ration out his love to his so-called friends.
Corporal Joe Adams, a man who tries to keep peace

between the two of them, finds his only security in army rules and orders. Private Tim Meadows is an older man, retrospective and contemplative, a *raisonneur* who observes the others from a distant but kindly perspective. After Peter and David are separated, the men drift off to sleep, beginning their interlocking dreams.

Tim Meadows dreams first. As in every dream that follows, he is God, faced this time with the first murder. Momentarily assuming the benevolent solicitude of both a military comrade and a forgiving deity, Meadows comforts the crestfallen Adam(s), returned from the Fall as if he has just failed to complete a military mission. "Ill-equipped, naked as the day, / It was all over and the world was on us / Before we had time to take cover."

Then David (as Cain) kills Peter (as Abel) just as David in his own person had almost strangled Peter, because he puts his faith in the pattern of existence and refuses to ask for certainty. As Peter says, we "question the need to stay, / But do, in an obstinate anticipation of love." When the two throw dice for God's favor, with an ironic glance at the gaming for Christ's cloak, David stakes his passion and strength against Peter's unwavering humility. When Peter wins, David strangles him while the Corporal (as Adam) is frozen by doubt and uncertainty. Cheered by Cain's confidence and suspicious of Abel's lack of realism, he is lost without the discipline of Eden. Cain's attack on Abel allegorizes the struggle between mind and the lower instincts, between divine force and the evil in man's soul, between suffering and fury. Meadows as God both warns and pursues, forgives and punishes David as Cain. "This can't last on flesh forever."

In the next dream David appears as the Israelite king. He orders Adams as Joab to kill Absalom (Peter) because he harbors a paranoid fear of traitors. "Do you see / That shadow shift? / It has a belly and ribs." The second episode deals like the first with dual personality, but this time it is the father who is split into mind and hand, dream and reality, rather than the son. In his use of the biblical revolt of Absalom, Fry dramatizes the oedipal conflict which had been suggested by Adams' failure to separate Cain and Abel. As a cheap, insecure, corrupt politician, David equivocates to conceal, as Adams had before, his indecisiveness. "Understand! The indecisions / Have to be decided." Adams as Joab is now as tough and vengeful as David has been. Peter (as Absalom) treats David's pleading with ridicule, then fear and finally contempt until he is brutally murdered by Joab, who cuts him down with a completely modern tommy gun.

The revolt of a new generation against the old one provides a kind of progression from cold-blooded homicide to political murder. The father David, as the personification of the established order, constitutes the chief obstacle to the aspirations of the young. Yet as in so much of Fry—unlike expressionist drama with its revolutionary impulse—the father gains the ascendancy, but at a terrible cost. As Hoel had died for Cymen and Rameses for Moses, Absalom dies for David. The king learns that mankind (and he himself) idealizes forgiveness, preaches justice, and practices vengeance. "Are we ever sure it's the victory? / So many times you've come back, Joab, / With something else."

The third dream moves to yet a higher spiritual stage. The ritual sacrifice of Peter as Isaac by Abraham (David) subsumes by its pathos and deliberation the cruel destruction of mankind which has preceded, first *ad hominem* and then in warfare. While revealing that Abraham stands in relation to Isaac as God stands analogically to him, the episode strikingly reverses the roles. David as Abraham has become aged and somewhat chastened, although he still has David's personality essence. "I am history's wish and must come true, / And I shall hate so long as hate / Is history, though, God, it drives / My life away like a beaten dog." As father of the Jewish nation which lies symbolically under his knife, Abraham now understands what the loss of Paradise had meant to Adam. As Isaac, Peter now feels David's rage for life. The scene unfolds slowly with dramatic irony, Isaac knowing something about his danger, Abraham knowing more (but dreading it), and the audience sharing God's omniscience. For another irony, Isaac urges his father to do quickly that which Abraham most wishes to avoid. It is the Corporal as an angelic *deus ex machina* who stops the sacrifice, directing Abraham's attention instead to a ram caught "In the barbed wire of the briar bush." Ironically Abraham suffers more than Isaac, but there is also a sacrificial substitution involving both love and death. The promulgation of new ethical values and the redemption of man through love become, for the first time, dimly glimpsed possibilities in human relationships.

The last dream, that of the Corporal, becomes a dream that all the men share. At the beginning, he is on a raft at sea, adrift actually as well as spiritually. However, his dream merges with that of David and Peter, and they become Shadrac, Meshac, and Abednego in the fiery furnace. The soldiers are no longer divided from one another: as suffering mankind, they are now united against the barrier of their own existence to self-realization. "Let me, dear God, be active / And seem to do right, whatever damned result." They are joined by a fourth figure, Tim Meadows, who answers the Corporal's "Who are you?" with "Man" and his "Under what command?" with "God's." Fry has called him "human nature with hope." From this literal recognition comes a deeper insight, a culmination of the previous roles each character has played. Adams has learned from his incarnations as primal Man, vicious lackey, and divine emissary to reject "the powers that ruin / And not the powers that bless." Through the futile repetition of pointless violence, David understands that "To be strong beyond all action is the strength / To have." Peter learns that the spirit may be transformed, surviving the perishable body. After the three realize that they are not to be burned, that they can stand and move and face the flames, Peter discovers that the flames are people. "This / Surely is unquenchable? It can only transform. / There's no way out. We can only stay and alter." So united, all of them have triumphed over fire, symbol of human passion, social inhumanity, and the wrath of a punishing God. What man really does in his living in mystery is to search out the ways of God, as Meadows reveals:

> *The human heart can go to the lengths of God. . . .*
> *The longest stride of soul men ever took.*
> *Affairs are now soul size.*
> *The enterprise*
> *Is exploration into God.*

To sum up, Fry has said, "What will carry the day is the belief that the good in human nature is even more powerful than the evil, if, with our whole hearts and lives, we abide by it." The return of the play at the end to realism, as Peter ascends the pulpit, restores the perspective of real life. As the action has moved, the scene has progressively widened from the rigid, paternalistic home to court intrigues, widening still farther to expose the loneliness of man on a cosmic stage, and finally deepening to reveal man locked in struggle with God on an inner field of spiritual conflict. The play ends with the striking of the church clock as a bugle blows, uniting the omnipresence of salvation and the bodily resurrection of the saved at the Last Judgment with the hope of a new day.

While the language of *A Sleep* is not exactly austere, its spareness and tautness reflect Fry's increasingly successful efforts to make his speeches responsive rather than capsule lyrics. To be sure, the dreamlike, other worldly mode of the play results in some beautiful songs, particularly at the beginning of new episodes, as in *The Boy*:

> *Morning comes*
> *To a prison like a nurse:*
> *A rustling presence, as though a small breeze came,*
> *And presently a voice. I think*
> *We're going to live. The dark pain has gone,*
> *The relief of daylight*
> *Flows over me, as though beginning is*
> *Beginning.*

As in this, speech personifications, the pathetic fallacy, the repetitions, and an invocatory tone appear throughout the play. But the verse rhythms are closer to the pace of normal speech, and the loosened tension of the lyric is admirably suited as a curtain between moments of great stress.

When the speed of the dialogue increases, puns, questions, and repetitions become more frequent. David, the most violent of the four, is most easily agitated. "Let me sleep, let me, let me, let me sleep. / God let me sleep, God, let me sleep." As for puns, Adam is termed "all sin and bone," and Adams asks, shipwrecked, "God, have mercy / On our sick shoals." Phrasal inversions also occur. "She's as good as gold while she lives, / and after that she's as good as dead." All these traits are particularly effective in conveying a sense of inner tension. Fry also exploits his characteristic habit of bringing in clichés, but with one term reversed. "I never remember / I ought to be fighting until I'm practically dead. Sort of absent-fisted." The effect is often novel and startling. As usual in Fry, aphorisms recur. "Good is itself . . . / Stronger than anger, wiser than strategy."

The interchanges between the characters have taken on terseness and heightened relevance, with the rapid-fire of dialogue approaching stichomythia at times.

DAVID   How long are we here for?
ADAMS   A million years.
    So you'd better get to like it.
DAVID   Give us
    Cossack and surplice drill tomorrow, Joe.
ADAMS   O. K. Wash your feet.

Although Fry has approached complete assimilation of the influences of others, a set of Orwellian inversions are notable near the end, when the characters appear helpless in the grip of outer forces.

> Police on earth. Aggression is the better
> Part of Allah. Liberating very high
> The dying and the dead. Freedoom, freedoom.

The biblical, folklore and political overtones are cleverly interwoven here, with a tone of jocular irreverence to fit the still-unredeemed natures of the prisoners. All in all, Fry's verse has become less allusive, easier to follow and plainer. The strained metaphors still appear, but less frequently, and the whole style is designed to reveal the striving toward mystery which urges on ordinary, fallible mankind.

By choosing to represent a series of biblically-inspired parables in a dreamlike context, Fry has achieved an unusual degree of integration within the parts of the play while he has felt less than usual pressure to make his characters real and lifelike. The final dream, which adds the mystery of good to the mystery of evil, does it by words, however, not by deeds. But the interweaving of the stories stresses evil and anguish which mysteriously are the human lot. At the same time, the double plane of action universalizes the horror of the action by revealing the soldiers as types, while pathos emerges from the revelation of the reality behind the role-playing. By placing Meadows outside the action as a *raisonneur* possessed of deific attributes, he has avoided the literal incredibility of the miracles and *deus ex machina* entrances which marred *The Boy* and *The Firstborn*. He neither affirms nor denies the reality of the action, while the verse is freed to full suggestibility by its lack of ties with real life. Although there is plenty of noise and clash onstage, the characters are more acted upon than active. As in Eliot, they are agents of suffering in whom is made apparent the truth of Fry's particular religious conceptions. As a presentation of Fry's concept of "mystery" in dramatic form, *A Sleep* is an outstanding achievement. The formal pattern of relationship, in which the three-in-one of Godhead is repeated three times and then merged in a ritual of community, is an aesthetically pleasing attempt to involve an audience in spiritual self-transcendence. Its most remarkable feature—and its most controversial—is the interweaving of biblical episode and Christian ritual with a modern atmosphere of empty churches, profane soldiers, and universal warfare. The linking of apparently archaic rituals of sacrifice and murder with the twentieth-century church by means of a dream of salvation is a striking piece of dramaturgy, simplifying perspective, focusing emotion, and crystallizing in a series of rapid scenes the enormous vistas of human anguish.

But the limitations of the play as theater are equally as apparent, even if we did not know that Fry has never since written another festival play. If the sequential episodes of dream life provide him with an admirable tightness and formal beauty, the play's content is so integral with its form that change in one would alter the other beyond recognition. Much of the impact of Fry's other drama springs from triangular conflict, as in *A Sleep*, where two characters, one active and the other passive, combine to destroy a third person. But much more than in his earlier drama, he will turn to the use of a central personage as the pivot of the whole play, as he does with the Duke of Altair in *Venus* and Henry II in *Curtmantle*. While *A Sleep* is his most existential play, a drama of "situations," he will henceforth concentrate on the more conventional "drama of character."

There are signs, both in the play itself and in its reception, that Fry was becoming more and more dissatisfied with the limited, highly intellectual festival audience that, as Eliot has wryly noted, attends the performance of a religious play more from a sense of duty than for the purpose of enjoyment. In *A Sleep* Fry has virtually eliminated the pageantry in favor of the "essential, direct emotion" of drama, at the cost of alienating part of his churchly audience and puzzling theatrical critics. Yet in abandoning the pedestrian moralizing and limited dramatic appeal of the conventional religious play, Fry has made a giant step towards distinguishing between what is specifically religious and what is not, between the essential and the accidental, and between the permanent and merely topical aspects of drama.

9

The Dark is Light Enough

The Dark is Light Enough [1] is Fry's most recent comedy, his "winter" play. Written for Dame Edith Evans, it opened April 30, 1954, at the Aldwych Theatre, London. A year later its New York premier was held February 23, 1955, with Katherine Cornell and Tyrone Power in the lead roles. Although the play failed to achieve the kind of popularity accorded *The Lady* and, to a lesser extent, *Venus*, it was still rated a *succès d'estime* and tied for second place for the New York Drama Critics' Award. The title of the play is taken from a passage by J. H. Fabre. There, butterflies flying in darkness evade all obstacles during their tortuous flight, arriving at the end of their pilgrimage intact and in perfect freshness. For them "the darkness is light enough." It is implied that the butterflies resemble souls guided toward a goal by a faith in something, but the precise identity of their guide and their faith is shrouded in mystery.

The Dark is set at the estate of the Countess Rosmarin, located near the border between Hungary and Austria at the time of the 1848–49 Hungarian revolution. The plot involves the story of the highly cultured Countess Rosmarin who dangerously overburdens her heart first to harbor the disreputable Richard Gettner from the Hungarians (he is a deserter), and then to hide the Hungarian Janik from the victorious Austrians. While the pacifistic values of the play bring it nearly as close to allegory as *A Sleep of Prisoners*, it is also as well-constructed as any of his plays. At the center of the plot is a double triangle complicated by an oedipus pattern. Many years before, the Countess had married her daughter Gelda to Gettner, a brilliant but unstable writer. Despite the probability that the marriage would fail, she had allowed her daughter to make her own mistakes without interference. After the unconsummated marriage fell apart, Gelda remarried Count Peter Zichy, a Hungarian who is highly placed in the Austrian government. In the play Gettner responds to Gelda's renewed tenderness, but only to fatten his own ego. Mistakenly assuming that the Countess loves him, he explains he had married Gelda only to "root himself" in Rosmarin's "radiance." Fry has drawn the threads of plot together by focusing on a homogeneous, highly-cultivated group of aristocrats who seem to know one another well, but no one else of importance to the action. Like Ibsen and James, he has concentrated on the social ceremonies which best define and reveal that class—homecomings and departures, anniversaries and parties. While the opening moments focus on a birthday, the weekly meeting of the Countess' salon, and the outbreak of revolution, surrounding the mansion is Europe as a wasteland, a chaotic moral void. The snow and frost in the background reflect not only the Countess' innocent noninterference, but also the sterility of ideological, nationalistic conflicts. In such a setting the spring blossoming of love between Thomas and Jennet or the autumnal mellowness of the Duke of Altair would be impossible. Rather the Countess embodies the ceaseless calm and serenity which are projected on the action by the house and the world of nature.

The Dark resembles many of Fry's earlier plays, beginning with the end of a journey and ending with the beginning of another. More specifically it begins with the rescue from death with which both *A Phoenix* and *The Lady* had ended, and culminates with the sentimental, obsessed attempt to join a dead loved one which Dynamene had initiated from motives of mingled guilt and resentment which Thomas Mendip had also felt initially. And like all of Fry's plays, *The Dark* begins with a number of absurdities, the Countess' rescue of Gettner being no more irrational, however, than his desertion, the Hungarians' pursuit of him, and the whole revolution. After a striking series of reversals which all the characters are forced to undergo, they encounter ordeals, unexpected passions, and recognitions which strip away their faulty rationalizations. The process resembles a law trial in which a number of versions of the same situation are presented, yet with all but one of these views revealed as illusory. Finally, love and death are juxtaposed: Gettner atones for Janik as the Countess had atoned for him.

Once again Fry has tapped deeply-buried archetypal situations, myth which lies at the center of the experience of the race. While Gettner's frustrated love for the Countess is a thinly-veiled oedipus situation, the Countess undergoes trials like those suffered in *Oedipus at Colonnus*. Like the Countess, Oedipus resists the demands of local patriotism and family feeling, persisting in his decision to become an Athenian relic. There are also striking parallels with Job who like the Countess is stricken with totally undeserved blows at his prosperity, family, health, and sense of well-being. In the subplot the conflict between Gettner and Zichy resembles the sexual and intellectual contest between Eilert Lovborg and George Tesman in Ibsen's *Hedda Gabler*. In both plays an unstable, idealistic writer-genius competes with a less imaginative, conservative bourgeois for the woman the latter has married. In Fry as in Ibsen, the artist has completed only one book, deserts the woman who loves him, returns to his first love, drinks too much, and engages in gunplay. Both Lovborg and Gettner lose the woman, but die in the presence of her alter ego. Gettner presumably achieves the ivy leaves Lovborg ironically foregoes, but a *Liebestod* brings the lovers together in a union which had been ill-fated in this life.

We are indebted to Jacob Adler [2] for his detection of close parallels between *The Dark* and Shakespeare's *Measure for Measure* and *All's Well That Ends Well*. Both *The Dark* and *Measure for Measure* investigate the meaninglessness of war, contrasting ethics and conduct, justice and mercy. Claudio is a weakling who would use his sister in

his own way to save himself—as Gettner would use the
Countess. Both ignobly, if understandably, fear death, the
penalty for a broken law. The Countess and her daughter
both aid the fugitive, as Isabella helps Claudio, at some
risk. In *All's Well*, Bertram refuses to consummate his
forced marriage with Helena, and the situation recurs in
The Dark; in both plays the admirable wife continues in
some measure to love her husband.

Yet the diversity and range of Fry's "sources" tells us
more about Fry's temperament than about his apparent
derivativeness: he is most creative when he is explaining
the "world" (a favorite term) in parable, symbol, and
myth. He is always moving toward the finality which
philosophy sometimes and religion always promises.

The main conflict in the play lies characteristically not
between characters although there are debates, quarrels,
and duels a-plenty. It is the resistance carried on by Gettner and the Countess in parallel, but inverted ways,
against roles which society attempts to impose upon them.
In her absence at the beginning of the play the Countess,
who majestically ascends and descends the stairs at turn-
ing points in the play, is endowed with godlike qualities.

> You know the Countess has the qualities of true divinity.
> For instance: how apparently undemandingly
> She moves among us; and yet
> Lives make and unmake themselves in her neighborhood
> As nowhere else. There are many names I could name
> Who would have been remarkably otherwise
> Except for her divine non-interference.

And from any objective point of view Richard Gettner fits
and even accepts the traits listed as part of his character
by the Countess' friend Belmann.

> that rag of hell
> Richard Gettner: that invertebrate
> That self-drunk, drunken, shiftless, heartless,
> Lying malingerer, Richard Gettner. . . .

His appearance, after being described by the Countess'
waiting friends and family as the one they most wish to

avoid, is a startling *coup de theatre.* When the Countess'
Thursday night group, especially the astringent Belmann,
try to impose on him the virtues of cultured society—
respect and gratitude—Gettner reacts as though Rosmarin's protection were due him.

However, it is the Countess who appears as spiritual,
almost supernatural being, even equated with God as
Gettner asserts: "God's a woman." She perseveres in de-
fending Gettner against all demands of family feeling,
expediency, resentment, conventional morality, and political justice. Like Tegeus in *A Phoenix,* Jennet in *The Lady*
and Hoel in *Thor,* he is an "unhappy fact fearing death":
he wants life as vehemently as they do, and his apparent
worthlessness only heightens his passion. Once the Countess has muted the uproar against Gettner from her inti-
mates, another, more serious crisis arises. Gettner, whose
name still "has the ring of reputation" and who possesses
valuable information, has just hidden himself when the
Hungarians arrive seeking him. Exhausted but clear-eyed,
the Countess is confronted by the reasoned ploy of their
commander, Colonel Janik, who is an urbane, cultured
geologist well-known to her. In a startling reversal he
reveals that her son-in-law, whom Stefan had impulsively
summoned from his post in Vienna, is his hostage.

> *If you give up Gettner to answer for himself,*
> *We free Count Zichy, and no further action*
> *Is taken against this house.*
> *Or the Count remains our prisoner and marches with us.*

With the appearance of Zichy in Janik's custody the
Countess' greatest strength—her appeal to Janik's consideration, moderation and forebearance—becomes her greatest weakness, and she becomes "hotly debatable ground."
Yet she holds firm to her convictions, echoing Peter's
words that "there can be love without evidence."

It is ironic that Gelda's defense of Richard in the face
of Peter's continued captivity places her past and present
husbands on the same symbolic footing. Also ironically,
the social catastrophe which is war, and which they op-

pose with equal fervor, has become a personal shock for each of the men who are isolated, even alienated from duty, wife, and security. It is ironic too, in view of the ensuing action, that another reversal should restore to Gettner his customary freedom to drink, blaspheme, and quarrel with impunity. At the same time Zichy's exercise of free choice will be curtailed, paradoxically because his civilized championship of freedom by others to choose—by Gelda and her mother between him and Gettner—demands the same noninterference which the Countess practices intuitively. Paradoxically, it is Rosmarin's pacifistic, nonbelligerent view which appears courageous and balanced, Janik's aggressive attack which seems shortsighted and weak.

The ironic tone established in the first act is extended into the second. When Stefan demands bravery from Gettner, suggesting a duel, Gettner prefers "to remain dishonoured without indignation." Gelda's expectations of affection and tenderness are then raised, lending tension to her inner conflict and to his.

> Now that you're a woman of uncertain mind,
> For whom sin and virtue are both
> Equally undefinable, I see
> You might be loved, more than sufferably.

Their kiss parodies, by anticipation, the love-death conjunction at the play's end. "We can kiss without a word, / A dead husband and a dead wife / Perpetuated in a sacrament." In many ways a contemptible Mendip, Gettner is torn by the disparity between his ideals and attainment, reaching a heightened awareness both of death's inevitability and the present meaninglessness of life. "The human arms can hold / A great security, for the time they hold / Pathetically, since they secure nothing." Gelda's kiss both here and later before Peter resembles Perpetua's kiss of the Duke in Venus and Martina's of Hoel in Thor: it is the kiss of human unity in misery, a denial of death's finality.

In another unexpected reversal, Janik and the Hungarians return. Defeated in an unexpected clash with the Austrians, he has been forced to find "a slight flavor of victory" in the capture of the unresisting Countess' house. Kind, sensitive, and perceptive despite the rigors forced upon him by his unaccustomed military role, Janik explains, "But apology isn't repentance." Although the Countess has been forced to move her retinue, family, and possessions to the stables, she has partly succeeded in fitting Janik's war into her own enlightened social conventions which, she says, are "reasonable, sensible and civilized." As a result, he appears more victim than oppressor. Furthermore, from the Countess' point of view, Gettner's desertion has become a blessing: Janik's soldiers have found unexpected comfort in her home.

In his meeting with the Countess, Count Peter explains his part in the recent battle. "I became the very passion I opposed, and was glad to be," an action patterned on Cymen's protection of Hoel in *Thor*. Yet despite his anxiety and frustration, Peter has refused to join Janik, for he makes war on war, not for a cause or against men. While his behavior closely parallels Gettner's, like Gelda he had asserted man's solidarity with men on a social rather than a merely personal scale. "I was, heart and soul, the revolution." Yet like Cymen he has affirmed life in the very act of wielding death. "There's no balance without the possibility / Of overbalancing."

Tension lowers, only to rise again when Gettner emerges from his hiding place sunk in drunkenness and maudlin self-pity. "My wife has married another man." When the soldiers comically try to avoid seeing him, Gettner kisses the unresisting Gelda despite Peter's warnings. But the Count refuses to act, despite intense provocation, reducing everyone to silence. The Countess then speaks of a time, long past, when her aged father had danced all alone. "It was dancing that came up out of the earth, / To take the old man's part against anxiety." The listening soldiers accept her invitation to dance, laying their holsters on the ground.

When the attention of all the others is distracted, Stefan provokes Gettner into a duel nearly fatal for himself. At the moment of supreme temptation, when Gettner has not only wounded her son but left him to lie in the yard without help, the Countess still pleads with the soldiers not to give him up to Janik "because there is nothing on the earth / Which doesn't happen in your own hearts." The incident not only provides a serious analogue to the half-mocking duels to which Jakob had repeatedly challenged Belmann; the Countess' willingness to sacrifice all her relations to save the wretched Gettner perfectly exemplifies the sacrifice demanded by Christian charity in the face of a Judaslike betrayal.

At the beginning of Act III the revolution has failed, the Countess' health has collapsed, and Gettner has fled. Peter has returned, sickened by the wholesale execution of Hungarian rebels by the Austrian government. Sensing that Stefan had acted as decisively as he imagined Peter would do, Peter now combines the Countess' compassion, Janik's selfless rejection of injustice, while retaining a measure of Gettner's penetrating self-analysis. For her part, Gelda has discovered, as Peter had earlier, that there is no balance without the possibility of overbalancing.

Although the Countess is dying, she is still strong enough to hide the once-vengeful Janik who comes now as a fugitive. Then Richard returns, having heard news of the Countess' illness. Having played the fighter in jest, he is forced to play the lover in earnest for the first time in his life. He has been forced to observe and ponder the fidelity of the rejected Peter, the forgiveness of the wronged Countess, and the disillusionment of a saddened Gelda. It is ironic that at the close of the play, Zichy, Janik, and Gettner play similar roles, each of them divided, anxious, and disoriented. Moreover, each is a self-discredited soldier whose exaggerated idealism drives him to self-sacrifice, a last desperate attempt at fulfillment.

In a final confrontation Gettner asks the Countess to marry him, believing she loves him. But she replies that "it would have been / Easier to love you than to like you, Richard" and she does neither. "What in God's name was it I meant to you?" he asks, and she replies, "Simply what any life may mean." With the Austrian soldiers at the door for the hiding Janik, the Countess dies. Gettner turns to face the Austrians, to protect Janik by going to his own death. From his own rejection of authority, he accepts maturity. He has moved from the "thought that good rejected him" to the recognition that "We're elected into love." By joining the Countess he has achieved integration of the warring impulses within his body. As Fry has commented, Gettner is a man of frustration, a man in search of God, who has said, "Reality calls for the sound of great spirits, and mocks us with our wretched human capacity." [3] His act of selfless atonement has arisen from existential choice, his affirmation of man's power to define his personality at any given moment. The value of life lies in "the choice to die / At the right moment." By being "elected into love," his inner insufficiency has been integrated by the goodness of the Countess.

Fry's language in *The Dark* reflects a new austerity and tautness, with a responsiveness to nuances of personality and situation which is new for him. It is still crisp and aphoristic, with the refreshing self-mockery that Fry often uses to puncture pretensions. The Countess explains:

> In our plain defects
> We already know the brotherhood of man.
> Who said that?
> BELMANN You, Countess,
> COUNTESS How interesting.
> I thought it was a quotation.

The disappearance of nearly all verbal symbolism, not just that drawn from classical and biblical mythology, is most noticeable, but along with it have gone most of Fry's plays on the phrases of other poets, both ancient and more recent. And his diction has moved steadily from ornamentation to transparency. The sound-sense paradoxes are much rarer, although balanced alliteration occasionally appears. "If you will be patient I will be persistent. / Within my experience there's never been / Anything so precariously promising." The puns, wild floods of invective, and excess of metaphor have also dropped away, although audacious leaps of imagery sometimes crop up, as "How many beans make five is an immense / Question, depending on how many / Preliminary beans preceded them." And Fry's penchant for repetitive wordplays appears as habitually as ever, usually conveying a strong sense of agitation, fear, and inner conflict as in Gelda's "faith in faith" and Gettner's pleading, "Lie, lie! O Christ, lie for me!" And when Janik asks the Countess if she has no thought for the downtrodden, she replies wittily but no less seriously:

> Not
> As they are downtrodden, but as they are men
> I think of them, as they should think of those
> Who oppress them. We gain so little by the change
> When the downtrodden in their turn tread down.

As in all his previous plays the lyrics are informal hymns to rebirth, one through violence ("rivers of their blood will flow") and the other through sexual love: "Why so shy, my pretty Thomasina?" Both songs ridicule trammels on fulfillment, one social and the other personal, the war song by its celebration of a bloody bacchanal, and the love song by the soldier's embarrassed replacement of a supposedly bawdy line. In his rigorous suppression of obviously literary and poetic allusions and figures, Fry's movement from verse to prose resembles Eliot's. The passages of poetry are still recognizable in the longer speeches, but the rapid exchanges fall naturally into lines of prose regardless of who is speaking.

The Countess Rosmarin belongs to a long line of traditional withdrawing and returning, benevolent eiron figures. Chaucer's patient Griselda, Hermione in *The Winter's Tale*, Farquhar's Lady Bountiful and Eliot's Aunt Agatha in *The Family Reunion* are only a few examples of the type. Jennet's alchemist father in *The Lady* is a male equivalent in Fry, while her sisters in the religious plays tend to be oppressed, moody types like

Anath in *The Firstborn*. Her combination of stubborn
pacifism with commonsense flexibility, of maternal concern with a rich sexual appeal identify her most closely
with Eleanor in *Curtmantle*. However, her confrontation
of situations of choice with an unwavering noninterference also resembles Thomas à Becket's resistance to the
four tempters in Eliot's *Murder in the Cathedral*. The
Eliot play in turn presents, as Carol Smith [4] has perceived,
an elaborate analogy between the martyr and Christ. Although the Countess has godlike attributes, suffers and
dies, gaining a convert, her completion like the Duke's in
Venus may lie not in her lifetime or in her flesh, but at
some distance in time or not in time at all. Her temptations resemble Christ's in the desert if we equate the
Devil's request that Christ turn stones into bread with the
appeals of Rosmarin's friends to her appetite for approval,
the Devil's offer of the kingdoms of the world with the
inducements to the Countess to seek revenge for Stefan's
near-death, and the Devil's attempt to make Christ throw
himself down from the pinnacle in order to prove his
divinity with Gettner's appeal to Rosmarin's pride in pro-
posing marriage.

Gettner's character perversely mirrors the Countess', for
he too believes in noninterference, withdrawal from the
world, and nonviolence. But he has been engaged in flight
from his talent, marriage, and human responsibility, and
he is hopelessly divided rather than whole and reconciled
like the Countess. Although he is a coward, defeatist,
drunk, and churl, his keen perceptions resemble those of
modern existentialists. First of all, he has realized that
man must die, even though he has found death unintelli-
gible. "No one has ever failed to fail in the end.
. . . / And very ludicrous it is to see us / With no more
than enough spirit to pray with." Secondly, he has seen
the discrepancy between enormous potentialities and the
finitude which confines his possibilities of ever realizing
them. When Jakob comments that his first book was said
to give literature a new fire, Belmann replies, "He fled
from his one book as though his own / Reality had struck

him on the mouth." As a result he has rejected all systems, all creeds, all rules. "Loving / The enemy is almost the only commandment / He's never broken." And finally he has failed either to communicate with others or to develop his powers without other men, becoming as Belmann complains, "a pest / Who never left us, and never loved us."

Like Shakespeare's problem plays, *The Dark* presents difficulties, degraded heroes and contrived solutions. From a technical point of view it is admirably economical and skillful, carefully alternating suspense with revelation, affirmation with mockery, pathos with terror. In the hands of a lesser artist, the Countess could appear static and priggish, a monster of virtue, but she emerges credibly as a gentle but determined soul, a this-worldly mystic not at all contemptuous of sensuous delights, but anxious that their enjoyments be free of jealousies, even competition. Fry's focus on her never wavers—even in her absence. Her great attraction for bewildered and unhappy people is Fry's greatest achievement in the play. Yet although she is sorely tempted, she has no flaws and no need to change. It could be questioned whether she would approve of Gettner's decision to join her in death as responsible, or even why she has protected him so assiduously throughout the play. Would she have done so, had he corrupted Gelda or killed Stefan? But Fry does conclude by condemning all war outright, not just some wars, a clear advance over *The Firstborn*. This is not an unmixed blessing, however, for the parable which the play develops nearly overwhelms the development of the action, providing neither fully articulated conflicts nor convincing support of its pacifistic thesis.

10

Curtmantle

Curtmantle [1] was first produced on March 1, 1961, at Stadsschouwburg Theatre in Tilburg, the Netherlands, in Dutch. Its production in Dutch would help him, Fry thought, to concentrate less on language than on structure. Not until a year and a half later, on October 9, 1962, did it open on the English stage at the Aldwych Theatre, London (partly to avoid, tactfully, the opening of Anouilh's *Becket*). It is even more remarkable that the play appeared at all. Except for translations and movie work (*Ben Hur, Barrabas*), Fry had been silent since *The Dark* had been produced seven years earlier, in 1954. In fact, he had announced that a play about Henry II had been "in progress" as early as 1951. After the opening Fry said:

> At times I came close to abandoning this play, but I knew if I gave it up I should probably never write anything again. I nearly have Henry out of my system now, and I feel I can make a fresh start. [2]

That Fry should have chosen the conflict between Henry II and Thomas à Becket as the subject for a play is not surprising. Although Saint Joan certainly leads in popularity among artists, Becket has interested a number of writers, resulting in notable efforts by Tennyson in 1879 (finally produced in 1893), Eliot in 1935 with *Murder in the Cathedral* [3] and Jean Anouilh in 1961 with *Becket, or the Honor of God*, [4] to say nothing of innumerable forgotten efforts both in dramatic and novelistic form.

The Tennyson play, as many critics have noticed, tries

to be Shakespearian and fails: there is the five-act convention; a developed "story"; and a subplot between Henry and Rosamund—a gross reproduction of the superficial aspects of Shakespearian tragedy. Anouilh's *Becket* owes nothing to Eliot or to a theory of verse drama. However, Anouilh is no less alienated from modern realism than Eliot or Fry, as the latter has commented:

> To try to re-create what has taken place in this world (or, indeed, to write about life at all) is to be faced by the task of putting a shape on almost limitless complexity. The necessity for the shaping—for 'making a play of it'—is inherent in us, because pattern and balance are pervading facts of the universe. . . . In the absence of any other household-god, simplification becomes a gross superstition. It gives the security of 'knowing,' of being at home in events. We even call it reality, or getting down to the truth. But everything that we ignored remains to confute us ("Preface," vii–viii).

All three of them use the stage, the characters and the story to demonstrate an idea which they take to be the undiscussible truth. Eliot takes dramatic root in classical Greek and the medieval morality plays, the Elizabethans, and the metaphysicals, with a fillip from Shaw in the concluding Knights' speech to the audience. Fry is Shavian and Bergsonian, while Anouilh has singled out a performance of Pirandello's *Six Characters* for its seminal impact on his work.

It could be said that Eliot's construction is focused and ritualistic, Fry's is panoramic and historical, and Anouilh's is musical and choreographic. This convenient scheme, which is useful if not applied too arbitrarily, would place *Murder* in a "theater of ideas," *Curtmantle* in a "theater of characters" and *Becket* in a "theater of situations." However, Eliot and Fry are both Christian. In agreeing to accept a being prior to existence, they seem less existentialist than Anouilh, Sartre and their French contemporaries. Like Becket, Anouilh's protagonists refuse to accept any standards other than those they adopt for themselves. "I was a man without honor," Anouilh's Becket tells Henry, "and suddenly I found it . . . the honor of God. A frail, incomprehensible honor" (114). When Becket says in *Curtmantle*, "What a man is precedes experience," he is presumably speaking for Fry or at least against Sartre whose brand of existentialism Fry has attacked. "In the main I find that kind as full of holes as a cullinder." [5] Man is responsible for life, not for imposing his moral standards on it.

On the other hand Fry rejects Eliot's contention that human nature shares in the evil which befell all nature after the Fall, an idea stressed in *Murder* by the chorus.

> We are soiled by a filth that we cannot clean, united to
>   supernatural vermin,
> It is not we alone, it is not the house, it is not the city
>   that is defiled,
> But the world that is wholly foul.

Fry sees evil as a consequence of man's consciousness that he must die and love for life the supreme good. "Dear Christ," Henry muses, "the day that any man would dread / Is when life goes separate from the man." Eliot has made his position clear in his 1930 essay on Baudelaire. Striking out at the "Life-Forcers" for their failure to show much concern for the letter, he insists that the spirit is not enough: "A Christian martyrdom is no accident. . . . A martyr, a saint, is always made by the design of God" (199), Thomas preaches. Only a formal religion can provide a necessary moral and ethical order (although Eliot's orthodoxy mellowed later).

Yet Fry has been heavily influenced by Bergson, Rilke (who was admired by Heidegger and Sartre, among others), and Kafka, and he has many affinities with Giraudoux and Anouilh, whose plays he has translated and occasionally borrowed from. Like his existentialist contemporaries, Fry is concerned with meaning in a chaotic society and apparently indifferent universe.

The conflict in *Curtmantle* is dialectical, pitting ideas against one another in opposite pairs. Ideally, Henry II, his queen Eleanor, and Thomas represent Empire, Love, and Heroism. Eleanor tells the other two:

Together, we might have made a world of progress
Between us, by our three variants of human nature,
You and Becket and me, we could have been
The complete reaching forward.

In his attempt to impose a unity upon the "interplay of different laws: civil, canon, moral, aesthetic and the laws of God" Fry mentions in the "Preface," Henry is opposed by Thomas, then by Eleanor, and finally, most disastrously, by his rebellious sons. This theme is worked out by the formal, outer movement of the play, which has the formal patterning of the Elizabethan and Jacobean revenge tragedies, abstractly conceived. Ironically, it is Henry's attempt to unite in Becket the State and Church which divides them, setting in motion the inscrutable but inexorable forces of nemesis. Knowing that existence is fluid and unfixed, Henry attempts to force an idealized rigidity of being on Becket, while retaining complete freedom of choice for himself. This is the inner movement, a second theme, as Fry has pointed out in his "Preface," "a progression toward a portrait of Henry, a search for his reality, moving through versions of 'Where is the King?' to the unresolved close of 'He was dead when they came to him' (viii–ix)." As a result of this imbalance at the center of their universe, Becket and then Eleanor overcompensate in seeking the same certainty of being, Becket in his devotion to the One, Unchanging God and Eleanor in her sterile Courts of Love. Their struggle both against Henry and the reality he increasingly denies suggests the more abstract clash of body and soul, politics and commitment, the irresistible force ("hammer") and the immovable object ("anvil"). Henry's downfall is not caused by Thomas' murder, but follows the restoration of a natural balance when the unbroken current of energy and memory resumes its course.

Thus the flaw in Fry's Henry is not a lack of heroism but too much of it, reducing his search for unity, law and harmony to conflict, anarchy, and chaos. "Not content to be one man and not the human race," he was, as Fry has described him, a tissue of paradoxes:

simple and royal (his nickname of 'Curtmantle' derived from the plain short cloak he wore), direct and paradoxical, compassionate and harsh, a man of intellect, a man of action, God-fearing, superstitious, blasphemous, farseeing, short-sighted, affectionate, lustful, patient, volcanic, humble, overriding. It is difficult to think of any facet of man which at some time he didn't demonstrate, except chastity and sloth (Preface, ix).

Anouilh's Henry, on the other hand, is a much flatter character, his childish fascination with honor balanced by the obsession with honor which dominates Becket. Like the existentialists, he sets his heroes far above the inferior spiritual position of the placid self-satisfied bourgeois. J. Dierickx says, "Anouilh's theater elevates characters whose isolation is the result of some mysterious election, some disturbing vocation—for purity if not for saint-hood." [6] This pattern resembles the opposition of Understanding Hero-Blind Chorus which Dierickx sees as a familiar theme in Eliot's work. But in Eliot an implacable, nearly immobile fixation on the eternal is embodied in his saint who "no longer desires anything for himself, not even the glory of martyrdom." While the title character in Anouilh's *Becket* (as in nearly all his plays) rejects the compromises of life in favor of an aesthetic ideal of integrity, Eliot's Becket moves and does not move—through a spiritual dialectic which resembles but is not part of the changes in the human soul, earthly governments, and the seasons.

In the Prologue, Henry is characterized in his absence as a charismatic, restless symbol of justice and order. A dispossessed traveler, Richard Anesty, stumbles into a group of camp followers with the first version of the question, "Where is the King?" His frustration and despair foreshadow the failures—in spite of dedication and good intentions—to follow.

The first act, covering the years from 1158–63, initiates the struggle between Henry and Becket. In contrast to the dashed hopes of the pious Louis of France for a male heir, Henry's enormous self-confidence buoys up his welcome of

Becket, just returned from a successful French diplomatic mission. Henry's anger at clerical lawbreakers is momentarily forgotten as he recalls his courtship of Eleanor.

> *I sidled in like an egg-bound goose,*
> *I held her in such tremendous awe, this woman*
> *Who had been the inspiration of poets*
> *Ever since I could understand language,*
> *And the haunter of male imagination*
> *Ever since I could understand sex.*

Eleanor his queen is the "mother woman," a combination of naïf and femme fatale who had been most fully embodied in Countess Rosmarin of *The Dark*. Before that Fry's comedies had been dominated by abundant, independent daughters of the Life Force like Dynamene, Jennet Jourdemain and Perpetua, while a near-relation, Martina, had appeared in *Thor*. Eleanor unites the down-to-earth practicality of the Jessie Dills with the vitality of the Perpetuas and carries as far as Fry could take it, the spirituality of the Rosmarins.

Alternately irritated by priestly encroachments upon his prerogatives, complacently superstitious about his union with Eleanor, and jubilant at the lack of a French heir, Henry abruptly appoints Thomas as Archbishop of Canterbury. Thomas protests prophetically: "Whoever is made Archbishop will very soon / Offend either you, Henry, or his God." As Thomas reminds Henry, a similar maneuver by Louis had failed, and he pleads his own inadequacy, the Church's lack of confidence in him. Worst of all, Thomas has glimpsed in the heedless Henry the primal sin of pride. He is trying to force, in the clear absence of any divine mandate, a clear victory of truth over error. Seeking to avoid both a dimly-glimpsed martyrdom and a tragic conflict of irreconcilables, Becket argues for a delicate balance of powers.

> *You're dividing us, and, what is more, forcing*
> *Yourself and me, indeed the whole kingdom,*
> *Into a kind of intrusion on the human mystery,*

Where we may know what it is we're doing,
What powers we are serving, or what is being made of us.

It is this equilibrium which bridges the age-old split in human nature: between body and soul, world and eternity.

At length Thomas capitulates, however reluctantly. But he warns Henry of the unforeseen consequences of divine will taking shape within and despite human purposes. Confident that he and Becket can "give England / An incorruptible scaffolding of law / To last her longer than her cliffs," Henry ridicules Thomas' qualms. Regretfully, the whole earth is not serene in his keeping. Only Eleanor, who shares Thomas' shock at the rush of events, understands that the security of them all rests insecurely on Henry's stability.

Once the erstwhile companions separate, William Marshal restores the commonsense perspective of real life. "What was one had become two. The simple and reasonable action, at the very moment it came to life, was neither simple nor limited to reason." Like the Greek chorus, Marshal not only forwards the action but serves as the author's mouthpiece, though more organically than the chorus in *The Boy* and less obtrusively than Merlin in *Thor*. Marshal also represents the consciousness of the trusting, hopeful common man whose welfare depends on the well-being of the King, who suffers his destruction, and who also survives his downfall.

After his ordination Thomas immediately resigns the Chancellorship, bringing the act to its most serious crisis. To his face Henry accuses Thomas of treachery.

I owe no obedience to a man who cheats my trust in him.
None at all to an ostentatious humbug
Who dragged himself up by the shoulders of the kingdom
And once up, kicked it away.

But Becket's roles have shifted and his stature magnified. Once Henry's confidant, he has become his judge; once a brother, now a father-figure. He tries to stimulate Henry's imagination with an ideal of grandeur and sublimity.

How, then, without rich form of ritual
And ceremony, shall we convey
The majesty of eternal government,
Or give a shape to the mystery revealed
Yet as a mystery?

But their efforts to dominate one another fail and they part, angered and shaken, the act ending in impasse.

In the first act Fry is less interested than Anouilh in rationalizing Thomas' motives for resisting Henry, although Thomas does deliver a somewhat abstract assertion of the church's mystery. Like Eliot in *Murder*, Fry does clarify the issues early in the play, although Eliot's concept of varieties of sin in conflict with good is replaced in Fry with a superhuman contest. Almost from the moment he is appointed Archbishop, Fry's Becket has chosen to identify his life so completely with the Church that he is little more than an instrument, its "tongue" to be "used in argument" between the State and Church. Aside from minor idiosyncrasies, he closely resembles Eliot's protagonist, although Dierickx's comment is apt. He finds that the Eliotic hero develops "toward renunciation, submission, acceptance, instead of violence and struggle; while Fry presents a man [Thomas] who is suddenly seized in a whirlwind of passion, after having however doubted his own capacities." [7] Anouilh's Becket, however, carries on an incessant game of aspiration, preferring to maintain a sense of personal integrity in the teeth of demands he be more practical: "We must only do—absurdly—what we have been given to do—right to the end" (114). He frankly rejects any conception of an orderly spiritual structure within the universe and insists on an almost romantic testing of his consciousness on his pulses.

Fry's Henry, however, is far more three-dimensional than Thomas. We become aware of his self-aggrandizement, his deep sense of family and personal loyalties, his furious temper, his passion for order, and his identification with simple absolutes. Fry is more interested in the man Henry than in the situations which inspire Anouilh or in Eliot's theological scheme. But Thomas prefers the more intellectualized perspective of innumerable alternatives to Henry's perfect conformity.

In the second act, spanning the years from 1163 to 1170, all the characters suffer in literal, ironic, or tragic ways the impending death of Becket. Once Henry has appointed him Archbishop, Becket is effectively deprived of meaningful choice, and Henry no less than Thomas finds himself trapped by the Life Force. Moreover, the bonds of society begin to fray as Henry blames his failures more and more on individuals.

When Eleanor and Becket meet again at court, Henry's vindictiveness has sharpened. Thomas has lost his variousness, as Eleanor notices:

> And you have lost
> Your genius for life, that ready sense of the world
> Which used to give your gravity a charm
> And your laughter a solemnity.

For her part Eleanor is now depressed and apprehensive. "The only way I can have any part in life / Is to stand and be the curious onlooker / While two unproved worlds fly at each other." Henry and Thomas clash almost immediately, when Henry enters enraged with the leniency of the ecclesiastical courts. "You lords of the Church Arrogant, / Like an old god crazy with his thunderbolts." Becket, for his part, opposes Henry's pragmatism with an affirmation of man's state of grace.

> And this truth is not custom.
> This is not under the law, but under grace.
> What you see as the freedom of the State
> Within the law, I fear, as the enslavement
> Of that other state of man, in which, and in
> Which only, he can know his perfect freedom.

Shaken, they descend to cruel, *ad hominem* conflict, as each attacks the other's pride, ambition and lack of vision.

In an expressionistic nightmare sequence, the focus widens as Men of the Court threaten Thomas and his followers with violence. At first relenting, Thomas stiffens when Henry produces a document: he is torn by the Hegelean dilemma, forced to choose between the state to which he owes love and honor and his devotion to a religious ideal.

Thomas characteristically identifies himself completely with divine power, refusing to submit to no other despite Foliot's despair and Henry's exultation. Forced to acquiesce in Henry's demands for debt repayment, Becket is no longer the witty confidant of Act I nor the tormented *deus advocatus* of early Act II, but scapegoat. Only Eleanor understands,

> *When the glorious battle turns into the vendetta*
> *The great issues, no longer controlled by men,*
> *Themselves take over command.*

In the second major crisis of the act Henry, having received news of Louis' long-awaited heir, announces his plan to crown his son Henry immediately and parcel out his lands among his sons. By ignoring Eleanor, who ridicules his disordered plans, he wins a pyrrhic victory. Completely disillusioned, Eleanor leaves with her son Richard for Poitou, there to "make laws for sport and love." Henry's plans to control Becket and make his now adult, illegitimate son Roger his chancellor are ironically dashed by Becket's escape and by Roger's being wounded in a quarrel among the legitimates. Troubled by depression and visions, Henry decides to make a tactical withdrawal, telling Becket: "The days behind us are thoroughly rebuked." Yet Becket is both resigned and suspicious: "Something tells me I am parting from you / As one you may see no more in this life." Once he lands in England, Becket excommunicates all those who had shared in young Henry's coronation, enraging the King. "Who will get rid of this turbulent priest for me? / Are you all such feeble lovers of the kingdom?" and four men leave to do his bidding. But when the full import of his impetuousness sinks in, Henry becomes a tragic version of the Duke in *Venus*. The King has paradoxically achieved the ideality the Duke has only grasped at and eventually forgone, but at the cost of the political unity and influence he had nearly grasped.

Sprung from a fraction of life,
A hair-fine crack in the dam, the unattended
Moment sweeps away the whole attempt,
The heart, thoughts, belief, longing
And intention of the man.

In the classical mode a messenger wordlessly confirms Henry's worst expectations. By having Becket's offstage death reported, Fry has avoided the melodramatic defeat of good by evil and balanced Henry's impetuousness with his idealism and guilt. The action also takes on inevitability, leading to Henry's progressive alienation from family, realm, and finally life itself.

The third act covers the period from 1174–89. It begins as the previous act has ended, in darkness and foreboding as Henry awaits chastisement by the monks for Becket's murder. It is another of Henry's trials by ordeal, his testing of spirit. In the last act Henry's vision of a supreme law will be ironically fulfilled by the same mysterious fatality which destroys his temporal power, steals his life, and humiliates his body. For another irony, Becket's once-victorious antagonist has become his chief mourner, having withstood "three years of it, the grinding of the thought, / Rat's teeth on the bones of the mind."

But from the isolated deathliness and soul-searching at Canterbury, the setting shifts to the hyper-legal, bantering abstractions of Eleanor's Courts of Love at Poitou. In a mock-legal pronouncement Eleanor finds love and marriage at odds, a repeated theme in Fry.

In love, the two images of life
Come to birth in each other's presence,
Creating themselves again from each other's eyes. . . .
Can this be found in marriage, where the two
Have soon reduced each other to plain endurers
Of a life already known?

Combining the roles of judge, plaintiff, and defendant, Henry enters to win his last victory. Against Eleanor's rational tolerance of diversity, Henry pits political and familial loyalty. "A man's enemies are men of his own house." Their grinding clash points up Henry's desperate futility, signaling his onrushing defeat. Obsessed by loneliness he reaffirms the justification of means by ends.

> *If Becket had wanted peace he could have had it.*
> *What's my crime? A secure Plantagenet empire*
> *And a government of justice. Am I to be*
> *The only man who goes begging for justice?*

Henry's corrupted mind confirms Henry's Faustian pride, his willingness to use violence to bring about the rule of law, although it is self-defeating, as Eleanor recognizes. "You, within yourself, / Are the one roped, waiting for punishment."

The final scene shifts to Le Mans, the King's birthplace, where Henry stands at bay after successive defeats by his son Richard and Philip of France. A change of wind has just destroyed the town, driving a fire Henry's men had set back against themselves. Henry's sense of identity, cut off from its origins, has reached the bed-rock of sheer desperation. Unlike Job he curses God and pledges open rebellion.

> *I meant the fire to save us! Do you think I kneel*
> *To a God who can turn a brutal wind*
> *To eat us up in fire? No,*
> *I renounce all part in you.*

Following the *de Casibus* pattern, the wheel of fortune has risen and fallen. Like Tamburlaine, Henry is struck down by a mysterious, invisible weakness resembling a *diabolus ex machina*. Stricken and helpless he grants the demands of his sons and dies, his helpless body stripped by the resentful, greedy refugees.

In *Curtmantle* Henry begins in a heroic human situation. In the eyes of subjects, family, and himself he is symbol, instrument, and mouthpiece of the power to bring order out of chaos in England. He forfeits the destiny he glimpses in a way that suggests moral responsibility to Eleanor and fate to Thomas. In the determination and dignity of his final stand, his sons' victory is vitiated by their mercenary concern with provinces and indemnities, allowing Henry a measure of heroism. Once self-conceived as a god-figure, he now distinguishes the futile dream from the human reality and reaffirms his dedication to the rule of law.

When Fry spoke to an interviewer from *Time* after *Curtmantle's* premier, he wryly admitted: "There are several plays there." In choosing to deal with a period spanning nearly thirty-five years, he anticipated a double responsibility in his "Preface":

> To drag out of the sea of detail a story simple enough to be understood by people who knew nothing about it before; and to do so without distorting the material he has chosen to use. Otherwise let him invent his characters, let him go to Rurtania for his history.

Fry's attempts to balance protagonists and theme are only partly successful, partly because Henry and Thomas are such compelling figures. Yet when they clash, they discuss issues or their feelings, and the action slows or stops. Nor is Thomas' abrupt change credibly motivated. And the most dramatic moments between Henry and Thomas—their struggle over the cloak and their last meeting, for instance—are reported, not dramatized. Moreover, the most skillful scenes in the play—the princes' swordfight, Henry's sudden arrest of Eleanor—deal either with minor characters who never reappear, or raise issues irrelevant to the play's outcome. And why Marshal deserves his prominence in the play is never clarified. Finally, tension relaxes in the last act, a weakness in many of Fry's plays, allowing long speeches and sentimentality to fill the vacuum.

In Fry's earlier plays, a protagonist succumbs to a blessing; there is no dramatic conflict in the ordinary sense. In *Curtmantle*, Fry has pitted individual against individual (Henry versus Thomas, Eleanor, and then Richard; the princes against each other and Roger), individual against group (Henry against family, Thomas against Court and Church), group against group (Church against State, English against French). By combining these conflicts with the inner struggles between the marvelous and the commonplace, Fry has stressed a central paradox of the play: internal coherence of personality results from an acceptance of life's diversity. Thus the plot forms an 'X': Thomas' stature and control over destiny rises while Henry's falls, the moments of their lives intersecting at the instant Henry orders Thomas' death. To an extent Thomas resembles Hoel of *Thor*, Jennet of *The Lady*, and Gettner of *The Dark*, all cast as martyrs but afraid to die. Yet Becket struggles far more aggressively than any of them, retains greater power of choice, and suggests far more convincingly by his demeanor that he depends on no one's love or support.

Both Fry and Eliot fail to dramatize Becket's inner struggle between pride and acquiescence. But by stressing the theme of Law, Fry has found a useful equivalent for the "wheel" of fate which seems so abstract in *Murder*. For whether or not Becket "willed" his death, his martyrdom removed the church's opposition to the political supremacy of the secular government. Divine justice has superseded human law. Fry's denouement thus involves moral values but does not depend upon any final resolution of their conflicting claims. Thomas' spiritual ideal is ironically embodied in Henry's social instrument.

In the pattern of its conflicts and crises, *Curtmantle* has close affinities with Fry's other late plays, *The Dark* and *A Sleep*. In all three the chaos of universal warfare, the divisions within and among closely-related characters, and the inexorable operation of nemesis characterize the action. Thomas dies for Henry as Gettner (presumably) dies for Janik, while Eleanor withdraws in self-exile as the Countess Rosmarin is taken by death through the same mysterious fate which affects Henry.

By utilizing a retrospective narrator within a framework of "memory and contemplation," *Curtmantle* closely duplicates the Christian mythos of *A Sleep*. The first crisis in the play, Henry's attempt to impose dual roles on Thomas resembles Cain's coercion of Abel. Interestingly, Thomas' allusion to "the deep roots of disputation / Which dug in the dust and formed Adam's body" closely follows Henry's allusion to the "poor damned sons of Cain." Once again, Fry has begun a play by allegorizing, within a historical rather than a biblical context, the struggle between mind and the lower instincts, fury and suffering. Later in the play the political murder of Becket as a suspected traitor resembles the conflict between David and Absalom in *A Sleep*, shifting the grounds from personal animosity to a more abstract, impersonal killing. The incident nearly coincides with the wounding of Roger by the princes, interrupted by Henry as Meadows (as God) had stopped Abraham's sacrifice of Isaac. And finally, just as Shadrac, Meshac, and Abednego find themselves in the fiery furnace, Henry is trapped by sickness and defeat after having burned his birthplace, an ironic "harrowing of hell." Yet Henry had "laid the foundations of the English Common Law, upon which succeeding generations would build" ("Preface," vii), a conclusion which Fry is unable to dramatize effectively, only to describe. Yet in *Curtmantle* as in *A Sleep*, the Fall, the Christlike sacrifice and Redemption are mystically represented.

Despite Fry's efforts to hammer out a completely flexible verse idiom for *Curtmantle*, some of his difficulties are apparently ingrained. He has made a partial return to the convention (as in *The Boy*) of assigning prose to the low-born and verse to aristocrats. However, it is reversed in the quarrel among the princes: only the illegitimate Roger speaks verse. In the last scene it is abandoned altogether: all the characters speak in prose here. Fry is best, as usual, when a serious, distraught, or pompous individual is placed among a more "normal" social group who ridicule or parody his pose. Anesty's arrival among the camp followers, for example, is greeted variously.

ANESTY   Have I caught up with the King?
JUGGLER   You're on the verge of him. Struggle on.
BARBER   Who would come to this place looking for the
        King, where we don't know where we are ourselves?
WIFE   Where we wouldn't be if we knew better.

Fry's witty, brittle humor has full scope here, as it does in Henry's banter with Eleanor and Thomas.

BECKET   I am content,
   Henry, to be one man, and not the human race.
ELEANOR   It's as well that there should be someone in this country
   To undertake chastity for the King.
HENRY   [*a pause*] Well, there you have your permission.
   Fill the office of my virginity
   And scrape a living out of it if you can.

Thomas' ironic humility is played off against Eleanor's playful astringency and Henry's shrewd, more political humor.

There is no question in this play of characters sounding alike: Prince Richard, for example, is urbanely sarcastic, Roger is earnestly studious and Marshal commonsensible and straight-forward.

When the action is concrete and vital, the idiom is muscular and colloquial. It has a theatrical spark and crackle which impels the movement forward. But when the language should be most taut, varying from syllable to syllable, stress to stress, with the surge and press of emotion, as in Henry's momentous dialectic with Becket, it is woefully pedestrian. The images are effective, but its rhythm is too limpid and static.

HENRY   The blessings I have already
   Are there to be blessed with.
   And the future is waiting to be blessed by us,
   In spite of the men who drag their feet. I can see
   He means to refuse.
BECKET   I haven't said so.
HENRY   I can see he means to.
BECKET   I haven't said so.
   But listen to the things I fear.

There is no connection between the distractingly autonomous tone and the (supposedly) seething, pulsating conflict beneath the measured phrases, no rise in tension as the speakers develop from anger to frustration to rumbling spite.

In the other speeches Fry's manner is often terse and striking, although it occasionally seems clogged and archaic. Then too there are glimpses at Fry's long-time literary mentors with the trenchant *Waste Land* overtones of "rat's teeth on the bones of the mind" and burlesqued Milton's two-handed engine: "the old would-be infallible Italian / Who rattles his keys of heaven and hell whichever / Way expedience turns him." There are also echoes of Yeats, the Bible, Blake and Shakespeare's "quality of mercy" speech.

> *Nevertheless, consider*
> *The nature of love. It can't be ratified,*
> *As buying and selling, an established commerce*
> *Between the two realms, male and female,*
> *By which they balance their economy.*

In general, however, Fry's language is sparer, more colloquial, and much more responsive than ever before.

Given the dedicated, Christian commitment of his audience and the suspension of *Murder*'s time-scheme between 1170 and 1935, Eliot could make rigorous demands on both his auditors and his medium. His occasionally slashing attacks on tyranny are stated in often dense, ironic imagery within a pageant-like form close to litany. Its particular angle of perception rests upon *revealed* truth, a truth which in Fergusson's terms is at once reasoned and beyond reason.[8] If common sense and observation conflict with the lessons of martyrdom, that is one of Eliot's points. Fry's shift of emphasis from Thomas to Henry results from his attempt to dovetail the King's historical character with the more abstract theme of conflicting legal systems, civil, religious, moral, and divine. This entails a richer sweep of panoramic detail, more psychological depth, and a looser kind of prosaic dialogue than either of his contemporaries use. Though willing to meet the demands of an easily-bored, unsophisticated audience, Fry has linked his brilliant, witty imagery to the whole play as carefully and artfully as Eliot has done. Anouilh is more secular, more radical, and more existentialist than either of his English contemporaries. He has adopted a sparer, more theatricalist form to focus on a simpler loyalty-revenge relationship in a chaotic, impinging universe. Neither Fry nor Eliot are willing to find their worlds as disorderly and shapeless nor the conventions of their theater as acceptable as Anouilh. For the allusive, ironic resources of their—and perhaps most—verse depend rather heavily, it seems, upon the poet's acceptance of an ordered cosmos. Within this diverse design, allusive and ironic poetry can extend man's minutest perceptions at the same time that it mirrors his incredible variety, as in *Murder in the Cathedral* and *Curtmantle*.

11

Fry's Imagery

Fry's imagery has usually been discussed in terms of either its cumulative effect, or as single images or conceits catch a hearer's notice. For many critics "imagery" has been synonymous with "verse." Accordingly it has drawn praise for its richness, exuberance, and freshness or blame for its glitteriness, emptiness, and superficiality. When Fry's imagery is examined more systematically, it becomes evident that Fry has provisionally revived a Copernican world view to mock or parody an older, more stable Ptolemaic universe, although the process has been largely unconscious and intuitive. He has been fully aware of the end he has wished to accomplish, that of representing what he calls

> chaos inspired with form: the multiplicity of shape, rhythm, pattern, texture, kind, expounded by one creative impulse. In prose, we convey the eccentricity of things; in poetry, their concentricity, the sense of relationship between them; a belief that all things express the same identity are all contained in one discipline of revelation.[1]

Psychologically the daily routine of most people is determined by the daily journey of a sun(-god) across the sky followed by a mysterious passage through the dark underworld. Because all men are subject to the law of gravitation, and up is a more difficult direction in which to go than down, men have associated ideas of goodness, divine wisdom, and light with upwardness. With downwardness they have associated ideas of sin, punishment, and darkness. From this obvious universal set of values springs personification, a perceptual world view, and religious images readily available to creative artists of all societies and eras.

But the more difficult scientific view—even if it is more "correct"—is that our platform, the world, is never stable: ideas of upwardness and downwardness are all relative and humanistic. Thus up and down, light and dark, and their spiritual equivalents, heaven and hell, may be poetically reversed at any moment, depending on perspective. This world of imagery is, as Northrop Frye has pointed out, "a world of total metaphor, in which everything is potentially identifiable with everything else, as though it were all inside a single infinite body." [2]

Fry's manipulation of imagery in his first published play, *The Boy with a Cart* (1939) is often rudimentary and strained. But it does reveal significant kinds of clustering by association which adapt his symbolic scheme to the dramatic action. The sun is the play's "tone-giver," merging into the mysterious carpenter-Christ who appears "carved out of sunlight" to assist the beaten Cuthman. His voice, we are told, "had lain in a vein of gold." Here vein puns on both *ore* and *blood*, suggesting the ritual communion of Father and Son as symbolized by the Blood and Body of the Mass. Cuthman has thus found a divine parent to replace his own dead father.

The episodes in the play itself are linked by animal imagery—horse, dog, and bird metaphors. Dog imagery usually clusters with fire (passion) and eye (sun-god) symbols when Cuthman begins one of his quests. For example, he warns the Fipps brothers, "There's one fire in me that no man shall put out. . . . I have the unsleeping eyes of a watchdog," the dog's tendency to bite, bark, and hang on suggesting tenacious human desire. Horse and bird images, however, direct attention to God, the continuing force in human existence. Although "God rode up [Cuthman's] spirit and drew in" beside him, Cuthman must still "plug" and "plod out his vision." It is only later that he "stampeded into his manhood." Like horse and dog, birds are sun-metonyms as the "larks dissolve in sun." Even in this early play Fry has made a significant effort to lift the action out of time and space onto the plane of the universal.

In Fry's next, far more ambitious play *The Firstborn* (1946), the imagery scheme is clearly transitional. A hand-music-dust cluster stems from the "joint action of root and sky, man and God" in *The Boy*. The "joint" implies both *hand* and *invisible link*, while earthly dust (of root) counters the *music* or harmony of temporal and divine. On the other hand a significant portion of the imagery makes up a cyclical pattern. The metaphorical alternation of departure and return, rise and fall, light and dark confirms the alternation of scene between palace and tent, the birth-death pattern implied by the title, and the thematic "interchange of earth with everlasting." Both image patterns are versions of one another, however.

The simple hand-music-dust cluster radiates myriads of synecdoches, or closely associated symbols. Their cumulative effect is to magnify sensations of alienation into images of universal chaos. From "hand" radiates metaphors of fingers, fists, arms, bones, fighting, percussion, sculpting, and striking. In a nightmare of desertion and sterility, for example, Anath vainly shuffles her "fingers in the dust to find the name we once were known by," and at the end, the still-deluded Moses tries to save Rameses. Futilely he calls together the five surviving characters as "five fingers to close into a hand to strike death clean away."

The imagery of song, keys, lute, loom, torture rack, voices, and words extends from "music." For instance Teusret's lute merges by association with God's vengeful bow, the loom of fate which draws the characters together, and the torture rack which tears asunder: "Our lives go on the loom and our land weaves."

And from "dust" comes imagery of sand, storms, dirtiness, cracks, and draughts, amplifying the search of Moses as new Adam for clarity in this "drouthy overwatered world." The process revealed in the cluster as a whole resembles Coleridge's "fancy," a creative faculty which

"has no other counters to play with but fixities and defin-
ites [and] must receive all its materials ready-made from
the law of association." [3]

The cyclical, more dynamic imagery of the play is organized by the rituals of sacrifice and rebirth. After killing
the Egyptian overseer, Moses had undergone a spiritual
death symbolizing the mass murder of his fellow Hebrews.
From the tomb which Seti's inhumanity has created for
the Hebrews have come poisonous mists, demons, and
ghostly voices. At the same time the inner conflict which
emerges in metaphors of death, delusion, and disease has
its social manifestations in images of miscarriage, prostitution, and incest, infecting Egyptian and Hebrew alike.
From the womblike darkness of Moses' mind the dishonored Hebrew blood rises to renew the land like a tide of
new life. With its ironic attributes of pulsation, nourish-
ment and decay, revival and drowning, blood is an effective symbol of nemesis. And because it flows in man's
body as the waters do on earth, blood can be projected on
the seas of space, reflecting as in *The Boy* the cosmic
"round of light which will not wheel in vain." As a result
the tide of divine vengeance wrecks the ship of state.

On the one hand then a fanciful hand-music-dust cluster in *The Firstborn* represents the Creation motif. The
dynamic imagery, on the other, reflects the human, natural, and cosmic rhythms, confirming the double issue of
the play, Seti defeated and Moses victorious.

The imagery in Fry's first one-act comedy, *A Phoenix
too Frequent* (1946), is organized by the rhythmic phoe-
nix-myth: a binding paralysis of life is released by a rush of
vitality. The spiritual tension of Hades and Paradise, the
sexual balance of maleness and femaleness, and the cosmic
alternations of day and night are assimilated within an
underlying system of recurrences: going round and round,
out and in, or as Tegeus calls it, "gress"-ing. The lovers,
Tegeus and Dynamene, want an epiphany which illumi-
nates "the apparition of the world within one body."
From metaphorical hallucination and dizziness they
achieve clarity and stability.

Metaphors of circles, spirals, and funnels like the spinning tomb, spider's web, whirlpool, and gales of dust all suggest the repression of lawless instincts by an artificial social order, "an oval twirling blasphemy." But Dynamene's religious, natural, and sexual inhibitions are all transcended by Tegeus' quest-motif. If the sea-journey is a life-metaphor, the flying phoenix-ship of Dynamene's reborn lover forms a dynamic counterpart for military bastion and moat, religious cloister and frozen landscape. Accordingly Dynamene resembles a spiritual Waste Land whose "dryness" is prolonged by the deathly impotence of her once-virile husband Virilius; the birth of love at Tegeus' timely arrival resembles the ritual "freeing of the waters." From a sense of personal *sparagmos* or inward tearing emerges the Creation motif. This archetypal act identifies the emergence of the soul from sickness to health, the universe from chaos to unity, and the phoenix from ashes to rebirth.

In Fry's first full-length comedy, *The Lady's not for Burning* (1948), three interchangeable motifs occur: alchemy, martyrdom, and seduction. At the same time the image-structure forms three dominant clusters: wet-dry, light-dark, and heat-cold. The wet-dry antithesis represents the dilemma of existence, all the lovers seeing their journeys across "the heart, the inland sea" as potentially disastrous voyages "on the planks of time" across the "swamp of space." Yet between sailing and harboring lie two symbolic dangers: drowning (damnation) and isolation as a castaway (ostracism). The inevitable setbacks which result from the multiple triangles thus emerge as shipwreck metaphors. Like the sea, the desert in Fry's comedies lacks the water of life, extending wet-dry imagery to the transmutation of wasteland to garden. As a result all the characters find themselves at some stage of the action capsized, abandoned or dessicated. While a dry, wintry or falling wind symbolizes the futility which arises from an inflexible, unfeeling society, a rising, warm, or spring breeze symbolically washes away social and personal drouth with rain or dew. The seasonal antithesis of warm spring and chilling winter extends paradoxically into heaven-hell, fire, and bird imagery. In an extension of the latent phoenix-symbolism, for example birds of spring, fertility, and morning like the dove, sparrow, and lark are contrasted with winter, darkness, and sterility images of the cuckoo "unable to die."

Light-dark imagery provides daily equivalents of the seasonal alternations, primarily grouping "good" and "bad" characters. "Good" ones like Thomas, Alizon, and Jennet "shine" like "the utter white of heaven," but among the "bad" characters, Humphrey is "swart." Ironically, Richard is "purgatory-color," indicating his immaturity and lack of origins. On the other hand, darkness becomes a "goodness" or fertility metaphor when erotic passion is aroused, and light-symbols are identified with sin and conflict when intellectual curiosity is implied. Thus the prevalent metaphorical descents into hollow darkness symbolize a search for the rebirth of love, fertility, and spring, as into the "mountain belly of time," emphasizing warm, pulsating eroticism. For someone who thinks too much, however, "altercation thrums in every granule of the milky way." At times Fry inverts the customary associations of day and night with light and dark, life and death, to suggest a macabre nightmare-world of anxiety. For example, Alexander is invoked with a "breast-plate of shining worms," while the fearful Jennet's last "silver night" is watched by a death's-head moon with its "white unmolared gums." While diminishing the macrocosm, light-dark imagery magnifies human perception of the cosmic, Manichean struggle of the forces of light and darkness.

In *The Lady*, then, the transmutation of flesh to soul by sexual fire, of wasteland to garden by spiritual rain, and darkness to light by intellectual enlightenment are all contained by the identities of the human, earthly, and universal bodies. Therefore, the cosmic rhythms are confirmed by imagery of fire, water, and light-darkness, which represent human sensuality, vegetable nature, and cosmic spirit, respectively and concentrically.

In Fry's next religious play, *Thor, with Angels* (1948), in literal and symbolic ways, the changes in human life metaphorically resemble the tensions between gray winter and golden summer, the grassy-green and icy-white of the seasons, stormy sea and muddy earth. Every new life, by coming into being, provokes the arrival of avenging death: life itself is nemesis.

As before, light connotes reason, virility, and health; dark signifies fear, impotence, and disease: in contrast to Cymen's and Merlin's "glare of the brain," the villainous Jutes are darkness-figures. Heat-cold contrasts also characterize, with Cymen spewing the "hot spout of indignation" against the cold immorality of his relatives, "the dumb icebergs." Another manifestation of nemesis, almost a parody of the natural cycle, emerges in the balanced attraction-repulsion urges of sun and earth. The male sun rises, spurts bloody fire, and brings forth vegetation while the female earth, with its muddy filth, draws down the sun to undergo a nightly passage through its bowels. The sun's phallicism recurs in such images as the thrust of sword into snow and, most notably, the Arimathean myth of "old Joseph's faithful staff breaking into scarlet bud in the falling snow." On the other hand, earthiness is linked with impotence and death. In *Thor*, however, the imagery coerces or even supplants dramatic action. Although there is abundant use of wolflike images, the sensational wolf-attack has no dramatic validity. And the divine light which breaks Cymen's sword and nearly leads him to kill his own son instead of Hoel is another metaphorical mystery which is inadequately dramatized.

In Fry's next comedy, *Venus Observed* (1949) the rise of the male sun toward the cavernous female moon is exactly countered by the fall of the male stars toward the enveloping female earth; the divine flight of fiery birds toward the light is balanced by man's mortal fall into a dark grave; and the struggle of chill enlightenment with heated purpose assimilates the patterns of light and dark, freezing and combustion and the alternating seasons. By analytic dissociation, "stargazing" symbolizes the Duke's

high-minded solitude, rationalism, and vanity; "fire-set-
ting" sums up the passion and humanity of his antagonists: his onetime mistresses and Perpetua, the daughter
of his overseer.

The tendency of sparks, birds, and thoughts to "rise"
and stars, angels, and heavy emotions to "fall" extends the
stars-fire antithesis. Thus the sexual contest between the
Duke and Rosabel-Perpetua takes its rhythms from "the
brandishing sun inciting the earth to revolution." After
the Duke "declines with the sun," Perpetua enters as a
moon-figure who has emerged from the sea like Venus.
When Rosabel finds herself unwanted third in the triangle, she complains of having "to get between someone else
and the sun." Not until after the fire does Perpetua withdraw to "sink away with the night."

The symbolic identification of the womb, earthly
oceans, and space confirms the transcendence of the tragic
birth-death cycle by love. In contrast to dust and watery
darkness, air and light complete the unity of "the four
terrible elements." They are also life symbols that re-enact
the Creation archetype by shaping the lifeless dust and
darkness into form. While a rising wind signifies a movement of spirit, a new life emerges when light falls into
hollow darkness: "an access of starlight and fish began to
swim." If spiritual mists blind the characters to reality—
though often bringing dazzling insights—rains instill penitence and divine sympathy. Seasonal contexts reverse
light-dark symbolism. Wintry whiteness symbolizes purity,
innocence, and youth, while summer fieriness indicates
sexual consummation. Perpetua is a white Queen emerg-
ing from a "blinding snow-storm of virginity," yet she and
Rosabel manifest parts of a single personality, a phoenix-
dove paradox. Strangely enough birds, animals, and even
insects are fire-metonyms while trees are darkness-meta-
phors, although in paradoxes like the dark tree with a
nightingale at heart, the power of fertile darkness is "ani-
mated."

The heavy predominance of imagery of light and dark,
of the heavenly fire-world and of angelic birds is dictated

by the motifs of passion, astrology, and rebirth. Like his plots and character-groupings, Fry's symbolic polarities are dialectical. They are not defined by material essence, but by their association with an opposite. His image-world thus becomes a plethora of interlinked, subordinated polarities which exists prior to any dramatic use of it.

In Fry's fourth religious play, A *Sleep of Prisoners* (1950), the imagery corresponds to the alternating death-rebirth archetypes: a binding or paralysis of the "Life Force" is followed by a release of that force's vitality. Within the world of the play, the forward urge and backward swing of the *tour abolie* and the upward thrust and downward plunge of the natural cycles are identified with the rotating polarities of the universe.

The prisoners' sense that life is a closed, tragic cycle is confirmed by hollow images of darkness, metaphors of disease, pain, and sickness, and natural images of winter, sterility, and deathly quiescence. Both symbolically and in terms of structure, "The future is like a great pit." Trapped by life, all of the prisoners seek the release of soul through death. Caught by their dream-state between life and death, they feel a dead Christian's impatience for the Last Judgment, which will unify body and soul. From the cosmic context of demonic torture, disease, and frozen despair emerges a redemptive water-cycle. All the characters must undergo a baptismal death-plunge, an underwater passage, and a re-emergence which resemble the rhythms of daily life. Man sleeps, dreams, and wakes—both literally and in the dramatic movement of the play.

The entrance or "death by drowning" dramatically parts soul from body, saints from sinners. Ironically, sleep, drowning, and penance are analogous. All those who fear the unconscious, nightmare, and hell use voyaging imagery to symbolize their isolation from a saving God. The second phase of the water-cycle imaginatively recreates the redemptive experience: imagery of washing, quenching, or cooling water "confirms" the reconciliation which ends each movement. The third and final phase of the water-cycle is a decisive emergence from the "mould of passion."

It counters and remedies the disease, rot, and putrefaction of the sinful body.

While the source of the imagery in *A Sleep* lies in hollow, dark images of water, the balanced opposites confirm the theological ties between the Many and the One. Thus the imagery assimilates the forward urge and backward swing of the *tour abolie* (dream versus reality, heaven and hell, donkey man and Nebuchadnezzar, the seasons), the daily cyclical recurrences (light and dark, fire and water, heat and cold) to the fixed cosmic revolutions (height and depth imagery, air and ocean).

As in his previous comedies, the imagery of *The Dark is Light Enough* (1954) moves on a double plane. To explain the transforming effects of her divine noninterference, the Countess Rosmarin explains, "there is nothing on earth which doesn't happen in your own hearts." Water imagery (the quest), heat-cold antitheses (renewal), and light-dark contrasts (morality) organize the play's image-system. However, imagery of fire and air ("upward" symbols), of vegetation, of animals and of the afterlife is rare.

Water imagery represents three motifs: a sea voyage, the changing seasons, and the spiritual life of the soul. The sea voyage, with its departure, a sea-crossing and the safe arrival in harbor, is like all life. A swimming image, for example, divides the strong from the weak characters. The dangers of an existential sea-journey, the second phase, emerge as grounding, drifting, and shipwreck images. The third and last phase of the sea-journey is the return to harbor: water, the harbor, and disease are grouped together. The entire cluster implies a victory won by the Countess through the acceptance and transcendence of human weakness.

The ominous revolution, the uneasy political and social *detente*, and the mood of uncertainty all slow the passage of time: "no heart is served, caught in a moment which has frozen." Snow is ironically both pure and sterile. Yet in contrast, the spiritual renewal which spring warmth suggests implies both passion and compassion. Forced to choose between Gettner and Peter, the Countess herself becomes "hotly debatable ground."

A third water-cycle, besides the quest and seasonal motifs, parodies the mythic "freeing of the fountains." However, until the Countess makes the supreme sacrifice, a sense of lost purpose emerges in imagery of meandering, shallow rivers.

The day-figures of light and dark (stemming from the title) resemble the seasonal contrasts of heat and cold, fertility and sterility. Light-dark imagery is associated closely with Gettner, who represents the forces of lost potential, chaos, and dishonor in the play. Not until the Countess finally decides to die like a night-light does Richard accept the martyrdom which is his destiny "where the dark makes no false promises."

The imagery in *The Dark* not only uses the scenic elements of water (or snow), heat and cold, light and dark, but it amplifies the spiritual fragmentation of characters and world alike. For this the personality of the Countess becomes an antidote. The play's thematic organization of imagery around the journey-motif merges into a highly effective mode of suggestion.

Fry's most recent religious play *Curtmantle* (1961) is separated from T. S. Eliot's *Murder in the Cathedral* (1935) not only by Fry's own early, derivative *The Boy*, but by seven mature plays. And despite Fry's early indebtedness to Eliot and his continued admiration of *Murder*, important differences emerge in their uses of metaphor. Recurrent images in the plays are similar: the Waste Land, seasons, beasts and birds, everyday tasks and the blood of redemption, an "under-pattern" David Jones has traced through *Murder* in some detail.[4] And both writers have conservative world views. For them the bodies of man, the world, and the cosmos are symbolically fitted within one another like concentric bowls or hoops. Their magnitudes may seem vastly different, it is true, but only to the unaided eye. To the awakened imagination, each is a microcosm or macrocosm of the other. Many examples could be drawn from both Fry and Eliot. "What is woven on the loom of fate, / What is woven in the councils of princes / Is woven also in our veins, our brains," say Eliot's chorus.

Nearly all the images in *Murder* are literally circular or cyclical in a larger rhythmic sense. In Thomas' mind the wheel implies theological patterns of rise and fall: into grace from life, into divine vindication from earthly injustice. The alternating rise and fall of the seasons, empires, and individual destinies are assimilated by Becket's wheel, visually formed at the end by the Knights' swords with Thomas as the still point.

With few exceptions Thomas' images in *Murder* are banal. Only for the priests, tempters and murderers who understand in terms of the reason does Thomas have the central position granted Henry by nearly all Fry's language: his stability at the wheel's center contrasts with the sinful waverings of mankind. In the language of the completely uncomprehending Women of Canterbury, however, Eliot develops the full potentialities of the similar, but discontinuous realms of body, earth, and cosmos. Balanced opposites such as light and dark, cold and heat, high and low are complemented with progressions such as approach and withdrawal, ecstasy and indifference, pain and lassitude. Moreover, the chorus' perceptions are almost wholly kinetic, sensuous, and visceral.

What is incidental for Eliot becomes central for Fry. In *Curtmantle* the King focuses and complicates most of Fry's imagery. Henry figuratively appears as both steersman for the ship of state and as the ice, storms, and rocks which endanger it. He is both physician and disease for the body politic, blacksmith and metal for the country's disused framework, harrowing Christ and infernal labyrinth through which Englishmen wander. He is rationalist and priest, unifier and divider. The ironic complexity of his metonyms confirms the enormous gulf between his idealized goals and his ruthless methods, between his failure to provide an orderly transfer of power and the viability of the legal system he bequeaths his country. Thus Henry is England's sun and its darkness, its water and wasteland, both traveler and roadway.

While Eliot's still-turning wheel is dominant, in *Curt-*

mantle the cutting and revolving circle recurs compulsively at moments of crisis. Crowns, nests, rings, skulls, and blood, a bullfight arena and the Eliotic circle of swordsmen occur at various moments when Henry's security and authority are threatened. And the destructive splitting apart of values, friends, and realm emerges in images of double and halfness: double vision and twoness of kingdoms, images, and worlds. The effect is summed up wryly as "redemption by divine arithmetic." Despite the orderliness and often striking relevance of Fry's imagery, it sometimes lacks the solidity and palpability so characteristic of Eliot, whose language penetrates to a core of archetype and ritual.

Fry's world view is not new. It is traditional and perhaps universal among poets. However, because of his metaphysical irony, the pluralism of modern literature, and the loss of status by poetry itself, Fry's system is only provisional. He has no rigid "chain of being." But the allusive, ironic resources of his—and perhaps most—verse depend rather heavily, it seems, upon the poet's acceptance of an ordered cosmos. The essence of his metaphorical system is a capability of transmutation: each image is both "being" and "becoming." That is why the principle of "decorum"—stemming from the attempts of modern rationalist critics "to get things placed"—is so limited and destructive when applied to Fry. He associates to dissociate; he analyzes to synthesize, regroup, and cluster. But within his world, as Fry has discovered, allusive and ironic poetry can extend man's minutest perceptions at the same time it mirrors his incredible variety.

12

An Overview

Among Fry's influences are Shakespeare, T. S. Eliot, the Bible, Malory, Sir Thomas Browne, Bergson, Wordsworth, Chekhov, O'Casey, Wilde, Shaw, Ibsen, Pirandello, Rilke, and dozens of others but Fry has said, "To be sure of 'influence' is always difficult. They work underground—and in listing names the important ones are often apt to get left out—as in making a list of Christmas presents!" [1]

Shakespeare's influence has been long, strong, and useful. The plays which seem to have had the most effect on Fry have been *Love's Labors Lost, A Midsummer Night's Dream, Much Ado about Nothing, Romeo and Juliet,* and *The Tempest.* Like Shakespeare and to a lesser extent, Sean O'Casey (who grew up reading and acting Shakespeare) Fry uses highly metaphorical, even metaphysical language, displays elaborate skill in vituperation, fills his plays with vital, independent but sheltered heroines, and mingles tragic with comic in a variety of ways. He has also used such Shakespearian devices as the creation of indefinite locales, panoramic if somewhat illogical plots, and the adjustment of mood to season.

In the light of often invidious comments on Fry's alleged indebtedness to the "wit" of the Restoration dramatists, his own testimony is illuminating. Considering the reasons for "the flight of poetry from the theatre" between the Jacobean and the Restoration era, Fry has commented how, the accent of living changed from the adventuring soul to the body's welfare. . . . In the brave new world, the Restoration theatre, the spirit becomes *esprit,* and as such did very well. But we have only to compare two comedies of a similar order, *Love's Labours Lost* and *The Way of the World,* and we see what has gone; instinctive apprehension of our nature; apprehending and apprehensive in the modern sense; we have gained verisimilitude but we have lost truth.[2]

Although the influence of T. S. Eliot affected the structure only of Fry's prewar plays and pageants and lingers primarily in verbal echoes after the war, both writers have been officially Christian in a non-Christian age, have been leaders in the restoration of verse drama to the stage and have adopted a similar concept of a concentric universe. Yet Fry merges man with the spiritual in joy, a far cry from Eliot's spare, ascetic, and joyless sense of discontinuity between earthly and divine.

But the influence of Oscar Wilde and, to an even greater extent, of Bernard Shaw, crops up in the aphoristic dialogue and comic character types. Like his great predecessors Fry is, at least in his comedies, an invisible ironist. Less passionately dedicated to putting his talents at the service of his moral passion, Fry has suffered from the same failure of critics to understand why he keeps making jokes if he wants his ideas, like those of Shaw, to be taken seriously. Jennet and Thomas in *The Lady* closely resemble Shaw's Dick Dudgeon in *The Devil's Disciple* and *Saint Joan,* and Fry's Reddleman and Bates in *Venus,* for example, stem from a long series of the comic uneducated in Shaw, Wilde, and the whole tradition of the nineteenth-century comic theater, to mention only a few of Fry's characters. But if both Shaw's and Wilde's characters are literary fabrications, wound together skein by skein, Fry's people reflect more of the complexities associated with real-life characters. Then too, Fry expresses a keener sense of evil and sin lying at the base of man's soul than do Shaw or Wilde. He also grapples, with somewhat more nostalgia for past, supplanted values, with disorientation and defeat in an increasingly chaotic world.

The Bible is another strong influence on Fry, supplying the plots for *The Firstborn* and *A Sleep of Prisoners*, and providing the "under-patterns" of spiritual quests and allegory (which link up with both Bunyan and Malory here), temptation, Faustian motifs, and martyrdom. Fry has understandably used the greater historicity of the Old Testament to a far greater extent than the New, but Wiersma has called *A Phoenix* "the world's wittiest commentary on Romans," and allusions to writers themselves heavily indebted to the Bible (for example, Milton) abound in Fry.

Like Ibsen and Chekhov, Fry has accepted the theatrical context if not the prose dialogue of modern fourth-wall realism, a theater which Francis Fergusson has placed at the point where Hamlet meets Rosencrantz and Guildenstern: the noncommittal 'center' of human awareness, the 'middle' of Fortune's favors, where the beggarly body looks sure and solid, and all the motivations which might lead to wider awarenesses look shadowy and deluded. Fry is unable to take the more forceful social tone of Ibsen, or to place so heavy an emphasis on the logical concatenation of events, but he likes the way Ibsen builds his symbols and his subtle mingling of tragic and comic ironies. And the habit of Chekhovian characters to reveal the deepest recesses of their souls, even when they are with others, appears in Fry. Both dramatists imbue isolated and outwardly trivial events with a sense of spiritual significance, like Fry's Chekhovian Chaplain in *The Lady*; both deal with the isolation of human beings and their tragic inability to understand one another; and both writers' comedies are, in part, elegies to a decaying aristocracy.

Fry's long-term interest in Rilke should not be neglected. He has summed it up in a quote from the sonnet beginning "everopening anemone" ending with the lines:

> We, with our shows of violence, deceive.
> Our lives are longer, but on, O, what plane
> Shall we at last grow open and receive?

Both writers stress their faith in the ultimate rightness of things, the attempt by man to integrate the divided elements of his personality, and a belief that love, like death, is an extension of human life into the infinite.

And the Sir Thomas Browne of *Hydriotaphia, Urn Burial,* reveals the same balance of words and clauses, the same fanciful mingling of classical myth and lore, pseudoscience, music, nature study, and magic. And a similar groundwork of biblical themes and stylistic traits recurs in both writers. There is a distinct personal individuality which appears in both writers, in diametrical contrast to Eliot's escape from personality.

Fry also likes Strindberg's love-hate relationships between the sexes, Pirandello's insight into the ambiguities between what we are and what others believe we are, the humanistic existentialists' emphasis on man's loneliness in both society and the cosmos, Wordsworth's primitivist interest in childlike wonder and sensibility in a state of nature, Giraudoux's fascination with mythic re-creations in unworldly situations and Anouilh's eloquent, witty dialogue in a theatricalist setting.

The range of Fry's reading and literary acquaintance is broad, but close examination reveals a preference for the romantic, the philosophical, and the oddly unique lying behind surface fragmentation or sameness.

Fry's plays all develop through a similar core of patterns and compulsions made notable by witty types of splits, doubling, and ambivalences. The settings of the plays are usually literally or symbolically divided, "poised on the edge of eternity," as Fry puts it. Barriers appear between villages, national groups, heaven and earth, society and the land of the dead, halves of centuries, day, and night. Most of the plays reveal ironically concentric settings: a tomb or cemetery surrounded by verdancy or an edenic garden as in A *Phoenix* or A *Sleep,* a sunken wasteland through which the protagonist quests for a parent-family-societal ideal as in *The Boy, The Firstborn, The Lady, The Dark,* and *Curtmantle,* or it may invert the tomb-within-garden

motif, as in Venus, which presents an ancient house surrounded by a forest within an indifferent, decadent, socie-
tal wasteland. Or in The Dark, a stable, open society
shrinks before our eyes under the impingements of a hostile world.

While the moods of the plays reflect the seasons, most
of Fry's plays begin in the afternoon or evening, rise to a
series of crises during the night, and reach their resolu-
tions in the morning. Each of the postwar plays except
Venus is set in a garrison state on the verge of collapse,
undergoing or recovering from civil warfare or internal
disruption.

Within the groups onstage, individuals are trapped in
dark, enclosed, airless cavities such as tombs, torture-
chambers, wine cellars, observatories, belfries, tents, or
churches. Or if not trapped, they may be ostracized, deserted, or actually pursued. Doto in A Phoenix, Alizon
Eliot in The Lady, Anath and Teusret in The Firstborn,
the three mistresses in Venus, Gelda (during her first
marriage), Gettner and then Zichy in The Dark, both
wives in Thor and Eleanor in Curtmantle are simply
ignored. More seriously, both mothers in The Boy, Doto
and Dynamene in A Phoenix, Margaret Devize in The
Lady and the Countess in The Dark have been deserted or
widowed, though still vital and passionate. If not actually
functioning as mothers, however, they become mother-
substitutes assisting the heroine attain fulfillment in love
and life. At the same time symbols of death—the stake,
pistols, swords, spears, knives, and guns—are all common,
but the insidious menace of unseen, lurking disease is even
more frightening: Cuthman in The Boy and Rameses in
The Firstborn are victims of unseen fatalities, both
Thomas (in The Lady) and the Duke (in Venus) graphi-
cally describe the body's gradual decay, the Countess
suffers a heart attack and Henry II a stroke on stage. On
the other hand, resurrections also occur, with the reap-
pearance of the supposedly-drowned Skipps in The Lady,
Moses in The Firstborn, Merlin in Thor and, by parody or
apparently, the "burned" Duke in Venus and the Countess in The Dark.

Beginning with the end of a journey, the plays often end with the commencement of another. At the beginning of the play, a death has usually just occurred: Cuthman's father in *The Boy*, a Hebrew slave in *The Firstborn*, Dynamene's husband in *A Phoenix*, a ragpicker and pimp, as well as Jennet's father in *The Lady*, Eccha the Jute in *Thor* and Henry's mother in *Curtmantle*. With empire in disarray, society disrupted, and family divided, enter the hero, usually a dishonored or deserted soldier, often a disinherited aristocrat: Moses, Thomas, Cymen, Gettner, the entire group in *A Sleep*, Anesty in *Curtmantle*. He is often thinker who fails to understand the Life Force, cosmic and futuristic prophet blind to the here and now, suffering wit, dominating victim of his own impulses, lover pointing the way to the tomb. Struggling with others, his worst enemy is himself. The plays then usually fall into three parts: an attempt at re-unification or reconciliation with a lost, dead, or deserted loved one; the collapse of that attempt; and the emergence of a new society as the protagonist's interests are shifted from death to life. Fry's interest in lost or perishable actuals which belong to the past may account for the predominance of rootless aliens in his plays.

The split settings imply the action which follows: Fry repeats, in his various plots, the focal situation of *A Phoenix*. A young man wants, or is wanted by, a young woman, but his wishes are frustrated by the resistance of an older man with less youth and more money. (The pattern has overtones of the Oedipus situation in the classical tradition, Adam and Eve in the Bible, and Romeo and Juliet in Shakespeare). Usually the older man's opposition is oblique or covert, his power being felt in his ability to influence one of the younger person's actions—to escape guilt, dishonor, or death. His body lies inert in *A Phoenix*, he eavesdrops as in *The Lady* or *Thor*, he arranges the marriage in *The Firstborn*, in *Venus* the Duke first proposes giving Hilda Snell's unwanted husband shooting privileges on his grounds and then delays the consummation of the young lovers' passion, or he impinges ubiquitously as in *Curtmantle*. The youthful competitor may be assisted by a mother-surrogate as Doto (reluctantly) aids Tegeus, Margaret costumes Jennet, Hilda encourages Edgar's revolt in *Venus*, and the Countess withholds objections to Gelda's marriage to Gettner. The young hero may ridicule or openly attack his older competitor, but the older man is usually converted or allows himself to be manipulated.

The quests for love and death in Fry are intertwined ambivalently, taking apparently contrasting forms which complement one another. On the one hand, there are the lovers who fall in love at first sight, blindly and unreservedly. Richard and Alizon, Hoel and Martina, Edgar and Rosabel (though not with one another), Tegeus and Dynamene all love sentimentally, committing the sentimental error of reserving their passion for one living being alone, rather than for all life. All these lovers, however, have dubious origins, finding themselves in the position of unwanted children faced by a hostile adult situation. On the other hand are the lovers who resist love, Dynamene resisting Tegeus, and Tegeus Doto, Thomas struggling against passion for Jennet, Perpetua resisting the Duke, Eleanor deserting Louis of France and—in the clearest oedipal situation of all—Gettner's failure to consummate his marriage to Gelda because of his infantile fixation on the Countess Rosmarin.

Fry's characters display a similar ambivalence toward death. While Dynamene, Thomas Mendip and at the end of the play, Richard Gettner, openly and desperately seek to give up their lives to somehow transform their environments, Moses in *The Firstborn*, three of the soldiers in *A Sleep*, Thomas in *Curtmantle* and Cymen in *Thor* launch the sort of attack on temporal or spiritual forces which may result in their ostracisms and even death. On the other hand there are those, like the reluctant lovers, who will surrender free will, self-respect and pride in order to save their lives: Hoel in *Thor* and Richard Gettner are most extreme in this regard, but Rameses in *The Firstborn*, Perpetua in *Venus* and Jennet in *The Lady* approach it.

All of Fry's plays approach a potentially tragic crisis

near the end, a point when as he says, they "must unmortify themselves," must approach and recede from the "point of ritual death." Love and death intensify themselves as they become clear alternatives. Only when the eavesdroppers actually confirm Thomas' blandishments in favor of death is Jennet moved to resist Humphrey's pleading to choose death rather than his limited love; the situation duplicates Dynamene's protests of love when Tegeus, dismayed by the disappearance of a corpse, attempts suicide. Perpetua asserts her love for the Duke in the heat of fear, only to relent in the coolness of penitence and clearer sight. And Gettner's desire for the Countess is heightened by her impending death. In *Thor* and *The Firstborn* Fry reverses the pattern when the eavesdropping relatives kill Hoel at the first sign of Martina's sympathetic affection and Anath refuses to intervene despite Moses' pleading for unity against the Angel of Death.

The ironic emergence of love from death, light from darkness, despair from festival, the phoenix from the ashes is coupled with Fry's habitual use of fires to mark the nadirs or crises of the downward movements of the plots: the burning Tewkesbury tower in his unpublished *The Tower*, the burning apparitions in *The Boy* and *Thor*, the stake in *The Lady*, the burning town in *Curtmantle* and tower again in *Venus*, and firearms both in *Venus* and *The Dark* are too compulsively repetitive to be ignored as mere conventions.

In the religious plays divinity is characterized as a ubiquitous, but unseen watcher which the protagonist, like Moses or Cuthman, attempts to control, but to whose will the devices he at last succumbs. In *The Boy*, *The Firstborn* and *Thor*, the *deus ex machina* intervenes so decisively that mystery is obliterated. In the more naturalistic comedies, however, the characters tend to react to supernaturalism with resentment or ridicule, as with Thomas in *The Lady* or Rosabel in *Venus*. Or *deus*-parodies appear, like the hung Virilius in *A Phoenix*, the drunken Skipps in *The Lady*, Meadows in *A Sleep* or the servants Reddleman and Bates in *Venus*. Only in *The Dark* does Fry resolve the problem by allowing the potency for interference to remain purposely withheld in the person of the Countess.

In writing tragicomedy which begins tragically and ends comically, Fry faces a dual problem: he must end the play either with the beginnings of forgiveness and reconciliation, as in the comedies, or with a *deus ex machina*, as in the religious plays. To audiences trained in naturalism, both seem unconvincing, therefore in his best plays he has frankly parodied the *deus*, or he has balanced the possibility of happiness and love with the suggestion that these values may be short-lived, illusory, or nonexistent. Hope and despair, death and life are ambiguously weighted. Society may have changed, but only slightly and temporarily; it is virtually certain to resume its course tomorrow. But as Fry's perception of social chaos has deepened, he has become ever less capable of visualizing a satisfactory social organization. Society in his plays becomes more and more futile, repressive and aimless, less and less viable, unified, and stable. Chromis-Tegeus and Dynamene in *A Phoenix* and both couples in *The Lady* go off presumably to form the nucleii of new societies. But the future in all the religious plays but *Curtmantle* has become the past for us. Even here the rule of law which has always sustained Britannia seems hopelessly inadequate.

It is possible to group Fry's plays in terms of the stages in the life of a redeemed society. This society in its infancy, smothered by the society it should replace, emerges in *The Dark*, for instance, where at the end of the play the newborn child's disgust at birth is amplified into an image of despair in the "contemptuous, contemptible" sadist and tyrant, Schwarzenberg. The destruction of Rameses in *The Firstborn*, of Hoel in *Thor*, and of Absalom in *A Sleep* are subplot versions of the same situation. Quixotic comedy involving an adolescent society still too ignorant of the ways of the world to impose itself appears in *The Boy*, the love affair of Richard and Alizon in *The Lady*, Adam's defeat in *A Sleep* and the failed marriage between Gettner and Gelda in *The Dark*. In a third phase it comes to maturity and triumphs, as in Dynamene's decision to hang the body of Virilius in place of Tegeus' "lost" criminal, in Thomas' acceptance of Jennet despite the imperfections in himself and society, in Moses' stubborn nurturing of freedom for the Israelites, Cymen's conversion to Christianity, the sharing of a dream of purgation by three of the four prisoners in A *Sleep*, and in Henry's establishment of Britain's legal system. The fourth phase involves an already mature and established society, but the only mature social groups Fry presents directly are the rigid, routine-bound city council in *The Lady*, Seti and his hypothetical court in *The Firstborn*, and the cabal surrounding the Countess in *The Dark*. Their offstage equivalents are no more vital: the quibbling council in A *Phoenix*, the fox-hunting, intolerant squirearchy in *Venus*, the superstitious clan in Thor, and Henry's quarreling nobility in *Curtmantle*. To Fry these societies are part "of a world which excludes the Universe and ignores the mysterious foundation of existence." Finally, there is the society which is part of a settled order which has been there from the beginning, an order which takes on an increasingly religious cast and seems to be drawing away from human experience altogether. This order first appears in the medieval village of Steyning in *The Boy*, which spontaneously showers its bounty on Cuthman and, almost to a man, adopts his church-building mission with enthusiasm. This world also appears in the ideal theocracy glimpsed by Merlin in *Thor*: "a ship in full foliage rides in / Over the February foam, and rests / Upon Britain." The restoration he speaks of recurs in Eleanor's vision of Poitou, "The great assembly of roses" welcoming her "In ivory, scarlet, and gold." But all these societies, like the ideally unified theocracies of Seti in *The Firstborn*, and of both Thomas and Henry in *Curtmantle* are lost or perishable actuals lying in a future for the play which has become a past for the audience. Although these societies should have been better than they were, Seti's loss of his son, Eleanor's ejection from Poitou, and Henry's defeat by his sons implies that they were better than that which has

taken their place. Fry's postulate that "a man's completion is not in his life time or in his flesh but in some
distance in time, or not in time at all" illustrates the
danger of his approach. Although he has commented that
"existence cannot be demonstrated, or even adequately
commented on, except by existence," in practice he presents a world in collapse or civil war, disintegrating into
small and esoteric social units.

Fry's admirers have emphasized the richly metaphorical,
open-textured quality of his verse and the joyous acquiescence in mystery with which his characters respond to
their inner divisions and perplexities. The greatest weakness of Fry's work is that it too often fails, like that of
Wilder and Eliot, to embody the form and meaning in
imagined human conflict. In using the commercial theater
to include areas of sensation and emotion which the theater of prose realism has rigorously left out as irrelevant or
unreal, Fry has relied heavily on witty, open-cast, often
dazzling language to shoulder the burden traditionally
assigned to plot and dramatic symbol. The most familiar
charges against Fry, over-simplified as they may be, have
concerned the supposed emptiness, superficiality, and derivativeness of his irregular blank verse, which had supposedly been exhausted of all flexibility and vitality by the
Elizabethans. Fry's drama is most satisfying when it is
most ironic: when the seriousness of his characters' problems is parodied by the whimsy of their verse, when their
miraculous escapes carry the aura of a nightmare barely
dissolved, when their recognitions of divine mystery are
balanced against the decay of the body, both human and
politic. He is so quotable that both his admirers and
detractors find a wealth of aphorisms in his work to support their positions.

Fry uses the theater to develop a theme embodying
what he considers to be the undiscussible truth. His antagonists tend to be weak or incredible, and his use of the
deus ex machina has been much condemned, and justifia-
bly so. Traditional forms of conflict—between man and

men, a group or an idea—are replaced by a protagonist's resistance to love, to the Life Spirit. The Duke in *Venus* rises to an acceptance of decreptiude after an emotional lunge at physical passion, but his agonies of sorrow and pathos at the loss of his wife are presented rather than fully dramatized. And at the same time Perpetua's struggle between duty to her father and her own integrity is short and unconvincing: her choice of Edgar, like the Duke's of Rosabel, seems gratuitous. And in *The Dark*, the Countess' moral courage is noble and intensely pathetic, but the dangers posed by Janik's threats, Gettner's instability and Stefan's rashness are not fully compelling. And we feel at the end that Gettner's unmotivated self-sacrifice not only negates the theme of love for life, but seriously compromises the Countess' enlightened humanism.

The best qualities of Fry's work arise where the characters' inner struggles—whatever the ostensible time and place—are firmly rooted in contemporary life. Either the moral conflict is fully developed in such a way that it cuts across most of the personal, social, and religious issues which agitate our century. Or it is articulated through irony—in conflict within an intensely divided character whose resistance to life and moral scepticism are expressed with vitality, nobility, and even tragic grandeur. Fry has incurred the charge of unwarranted optimism mainly because of works in which the full impact of evil and decay fail to contribute much to the final recognitions and denouement. Yet except for *The Boy, A Phoenix*, the last part of *A Sleep* and, more wryly, *The Lady*, none of his plays ends happily. His others end with the death either of a young, bewildered innocent as in *The Firstborn*, and *Thor*, or of major characters in *The Dark* and *Curtmantle*, or in the destruction of societies in *The Firstborn, The Dark* and *Curtmantle*, or in the postponement of visionary schemes of world betterment. There is much smoldering resentment, resignation, or even barely concealed despair beneath the narrow escapes which his characters make into faith.

Fry's saints are those like Cymen in *Thor*, the Duke in

Venus, the Countess in *The Dark* and Thomas in *Curt-mantle* who affirm a hard-won maturity of delight, a fervent advocacy of cosmic dialectics, an active patience declaring the solvency of good. Sin and evil appear in Fry, as they do not in Shaw, but in contexts that qualify their importance. Fry has been unwilling to accept the limitations of traditional forms of comedy which uphold a rational, social norm against an individual's repetitive obsessions. The overcoming of sin and evil is less important to him than the gentle ridicule of a lack of self-knowledge. His saints are dedicated to transformation of life by noninterference, to lessening perverse resistance to the healing Life Force, to bringing hope and joy to suffering mankind. Their function is to be primarily charismatic, tolerant, high-minded, and ubiquitously merciful, revealing their influence primarily through the regard in which other characters hold them.

When irony is interfused with theme, Fry's vision is most satisfying. Much of the comic effect of *A Phoenix* consists in the fact that life springs from death, that the trammels of lethargic systems and deathly values sharpen the contention of death with life, evil with good, and desolation with delight. In *The Lady* we are intensely aware that the pastoral, idyllic ceremonies of prayer, festival, and marriage cannot obviate either the liveliness or the menace of human passions, social urges for transformation, or natural and cosmic cataclysms. And in *A Sleep*, the infinite variety of human creativity and the evolution of humanity from partial to full inclusion of unity are balanced against seething hates, mechanistic habits, and stubborn prejudices. The simple, enormously appealing unity of affection which animates Dynamene and Tegeus, the paired lovers in *The Lady*, and the prisoners in *A Sleep* is priceless, but Fry offers the villainous insensitivity of Virilius, the lusts and greeds of Tyson and Humphrey, and the hateful insecurity of David as reminders that life in any era can be stultified by System. While the courageous characters endure the apparent meaninglessness through praise of life, others suffer and cause pain through failure to accept the mystery of joy. In Fry's later work this balance of the experience of tragedy and the intuition of comedy becomes harder and harder to sustain. His societies are more prone to disintegration as social values are replaced by arbitrary, dictatorial governments which rule by repression or opportunism. Social units become small and esoteric, like the Duke of Altair's isolated manor, the Countess' outpost of culture and Eleanor's Court of Love. Or they may even be confined to a single individual, with faithful but helpless retainer, comic versions of Lear on the heath like the Duke and Reedbeck, or Henry's son Roger and William Marshal. The world of the awakened critical intelligence which Fry sustained in A *Phoenix* and *The Lady* has been replaced by secret and sheltered places, a mood of romance, a sense of individual detachment from routine existence.

While Fry is less naïvely optimistic than he usually is thought to be and while his best works portray extremely penetrating dissections of human feeling, his outlook on life is affirmative. He does not, like Eliot, view the isolated self in our time with austerity and bitterness. On the other hand the sentimental belief in unalloyed human goodness is a partial view belonging to one or another of Fry's characters, rather than reflecting the whole of the author's viewpoint. But Fry avoids the corrosive, biting satire of a Swift or Brecht that seems at times to despair at reform, so abysmal does man's degradation appear.

Fry views life as wildly unprosaic, as whole and wondrous. Our inability to comprehend either a microbe or the solar system should result neither in paralyzing anxiety nor blissful affirmation, but in a provisional groping towards maturity and individual self-knowledge. While trying to avoid looking for new ways to approach old trivialities, Fry does find permanence in such traditional values as love, responsibility, justice, forgiveness, and duty, but they are positive commitments to participation in society. He certainly advocates freedom from physical and social restraints which destroy human openness to sensation and emotion, and he believes that even the commonplace events of life reveal an incarnate spirit. The ideal play should reach a point where persons and events have a recognizable ring of old truth, and yet seem to occur in a lightening spasm of discovery.

Unlike T. S. Eliot, Arthur Miller or Pirandello, for example, Fry has never identified himself with either organized religion or an ideology of government. But he belongs to the protestant tradition which holds that an individual should be free to make his own moral choices without regard to dogma or creed, but with responsibility to them in accord with his views of love, compassion, and mercy. He responds more fully to the intuitive authority of the heart than to the authority of tradition and learning, even if his thought becomes a little fuzzy and unsystematic in the process. Neither is Fry an existentialist, despite his deep and long-lasting admiration for Bergson and Rilke. He stresses the need for integrity in the face of serious temptations to compromise, but subjectivity in his plays is always subject to rationality. Then too, death, dread, and failure, which so pervade the thought of such existentialists as Heidegger, Jaspers and Sartre, give way to joy, exultation and sensuous exuberance in Fry. He believes that man integrates his disparate impulses through purposeful life within a human community, striving at all times for unity with an imminent, personal God. This partly accounts for the absence or parody of social doctrine in Fry's work, his "I demand justice for the criminal classes!" in *The Lady* or "Reedbequity" in *Venus* or the Countess' warnings of a time when "the downtrodden in turn tread down." His characters respond less to the influence of heredity, social institutions, or glands than to supratemporal forces such as free will and destiny. His characters thus either love blindly, unconsciously, and sentimentally, failing to rise to the love of all created beings which the Life Force demands, or they resist either form of love, only to "succumb to a blessing," as Mandel puts it.

Unlike most of his contemporaries, Fry has not given man's meanness, animality, and evil a central position in his work. If men are selfish, egoistic, and blind to love, it belongs to his more enlightened, self-controlled, and discerning characters to bring their understanding and tolerance to bear upon the pain and anguish that results. Although greed and lust have not been conquered in *The Lady*, the greedy and lustful Tyson and Humphrey have been held up to ridicule and ultimately chastened. Duplicity, decay, and death are still evils at the end of *Venus*, but the Duke can find joy even in the painful sensations of old age. Fry has occasionally seemed wordy, sentimental, and lacking in conventional kinds of conflict, but he has more than compensated with vital and compassionate characters, the courage to deal with contemporary human conflicts and issues, and some of the most vital language in the theater today.

Notes

1 Outlook and Ideas

1. "The Verse of Christopher Fry," *Scrutiny*, XVIII (June 1951), p. 81.

2. "Notes on English Verse Drama: Christopher Fry," *Hudson Review*, II, no. 2 (Summer 1950), p. 208.

3. *An Experience of Critics* (London, 1952), p. 23.

4. *Christopher Fry: An Appreciation* (London, 1952), p. 28.

5. *An Experience*, p. 23.

6. "Venus Considered," *Theatre Newsletter* (11 March 1950).

7. (New York, 1966), p. 120.

8. *Adelphi*, XXVII (November 1950), 27–29. The essay was reprinted in *Tulane Drama Review*, IV (March 1960), 77–79.

9. "Letters to an Actor Playing Hamlet," *Shakespeare Survey*, ed. Allardyce Nicoll (Cambridge, 1952), p. 58.

10. "The Comic Victim-Victor," *The Drama of Comedy* (Richmond, Va., 1966).

11. "The Play of Ideas," *New Statesman and Nation* (22 April, 1950), p. 458.

12. *Ibid*.

13. "On Keeping the Sense of Wonder," *Vogue*, CXXVII (January, 1956), p. 158.

14. "Why Verse," *Vogue*, CXXV (March 1, 1955), p. 166.

15. *Ibid*.

16. "The Play of Ideas," *op. cit.*

2   *The Boy with a Cart*

1. London, 1939.
2. In *Collected Plays* (London, 1963), p. 152.

3   *The Firstborn*

1. London, 1958.
2. (London, 1946), p. 14.
3. *An Experience of Critics*, p. 32.
4. *Ibid.*, p. 31.

4   A Phoenix too Frequent

1. "Author's Struggle," (February 6, 1955), *The New York Times*, Sec. II, 3:1.
2. London, 1946.
3. "Headpiece," *Christian Drama*, II (June 1951), p. i.
4. Quoted Eric Johns, "Poet's Playhouse," *Theatre World*, XLIV (February, 1948), p. 28.
5. Letter to the Author, April 1, 1964.
6. "Venus Considered," *Theatre Newsletter* (11 March, 1950).
7. Jeremy Taylor, *The Rule and Exercises of Holy Dying* (London, 1894), 162–63, and *The Satyricon of Petronius Arbiter*, trans. William Burnaby (New York, n.d.), pp. 172–76.
8. Letters to the Author dated December 3, 1963 and April 1, 1964.
9. *The Drama of Chekhov, Synge, Yeats and Pirandello* (London, 1963), p. 169.
10. Stanley Wiersma has found references to phrases in chapters 5–8 in Paul's "Epistle to the Romans" scattered through the play, with particular stress on a line in the third paragraph of Romans 6: "The wages of sin is death, but the gift of God is eternal life through Jesus Christ our Lord." "*Phoenix* is," he concludes, "the world's wittiest commentary on Romans."
11. Letter to the Author, December 3, 1963.

5   *The Lady's not for Burning*

1. London, 1949.
2. "The Author Explains," *World Review* (June 1949), p. 21.

3. "Christopher Fry and the Redemption of Joy," *Vanderbilt Studies in the Humanities,* I (1951), p. 19.

4. "Eliot, Fry and Broadway," *Arizona Quarterly,* XI, (Winter 1955), p. 345.

6 Thor, with Angels

1. London, 1948.

7 Venus Obscrved

1. London, 1949.

2. "Venus Considered," *op. cit.*

3. Letter to the Author, Dec. 3, 1963.

4. "Preface," *Ring Round the Moon* (London, 1951).

5. My translation, *Pieces Brillantes* (Paris, 1951), pp. 226–27.

6. *Psychiatric Dictionary,* eds. L. E. Hensie and R. J. Campbell, 3rd edition (New York, 1960).

7. "Venus Considered," *op. cit.*

8 A Sleep of Prisoners

1. New York, 1951.

2. "Drama in a House of Worship," *The New York Times,* Sec. II (October 14, 1951), p. 2.

9 The Dark is Light Enough

1. New York, 1954.

2. "Shakespeare and Christopher Fry," *Educational Theatre Journal* (1959), 85–98.

3. "Author's Struggle," *op. cit.*

4. Carol Smith, *T. S. Eliot's Dramatic Theory and Practice* (Princeton, 1963).

10 Curtmantle

1. New York, 1961.

2. "Theatre Abroad: Return of the Phoenix," *Time* LXXVII (10 March 1961), p. 86.

3. In *The Complete Poems and Plays: 1909–1950* (New York, 1958), 173–221.

4. Trans. Lucienne Hill (New York, 1964).

5. Letter to the Author, April 1, 1964.

6. "King and Archbishop: Henry II and Becket from Ten-

nyson to Fry," *Revue des Langues Vivantes*, XXVIII (1961–62), p. 428.

7. *Ibid.*

8. *The Idea of a Theatre* (Princeton, 1949), p. 220.

11   Fry's Imagery

1. "Why Verse?" *op. cit.*, p. 137.

2. *An Anatomy of Criticism* (Princeton, 1957), p. 136.

3. "The Imagination," *Criticism: The Major Texts*, ed. W. J. Bate (Cambridge, Mass., 1953), p. 38.

4. *The Plays of T. S. Eliot* (London, 1960), p. 17.

12   An Overview

1. Letter to the Author, December 3, 1963.

2. "Poetry and the Theatre," *Adam*, XIX (1951), pp. 214–15.

Selected Bibliography

Adler, Jacob H. "Shakespeare and Christopher Fry," *Educational Theatre Journal*, XI (May 1959), pp. 85–98.

Alexander, John. "Christopher Fry and Religious Comedy," *Meanjin*, XV (Autumn 1956), pp. 77–81.

Arrowsmith, Martin. "Notes on English Verse Drama: Christopher Fry," *Hudson Review*, III (Summer 1950), 203–16.

Bewley, Marius. "The Verse of Christopher Fry," *Scrutiny*, XVIII (June 1951), 78–84.

Dobrée, Bonamy. "Some London Plays," *The Sewanee Review*, LXIII (Spring 1955), 270–80.

Donoghue, Denis. "Christopher Fry's Theatre of Words." In *The Third Voice: Modern British and American Verse Drama*. Princeton, 1959.

Lecky, Eleazer. "Mystery in the Plays of Christopher Fry," *Tulane Drama Review*, IV (Spring 1960), 80–87.

Mandel, O. "Theme in the Drama of Christopher Fry," *Etudes Anglaises*, X (Oct.–Dec. 1957), 335–49.

Spears, Monroe K. "Christopher Fry and the Redemption of Joy," *Poetry*, LXXVIII (April 1951), 23–43. Reprinted in *Vanderbilt Studies in the Humanities*, I.

Spender, Stephen. "Christopher Fry," *The Spectator*, CLXXXIV (March 24, 1950), 364.

Stanford, Derek. *Christopher Fry: An Appreciation*. London, 1951.

Vos. Nelvin. "The Comic Victim-Victor," *The Drama of Comedy: Victim and Victor*. Richmond, Va., 1966.

Williams, Raymond. "Christopher Fry," *Drama from Ibsen to Eliot*. London, 1952.

Note: A more complete bibliography has been compiled by Bernice Schear and Eugene Prater, "A Bibliography on Christopher Fry," *Tulane Drama Review*, IV (March 1960), pp. 88–98.

Index

Anouilh, Jean: inventiveness, 17; and Fry, 63; *Ring Round the Moon* trans. by Fry, 83; *Madame Colombe* and *Venus*, 88–89; *Becket* and *Curtmantle*, 122–23, 129, 139; influence on Fry, 156

Auden, W. H.: influence on *Boy*, 36; and *Lady*, 72; and *Venus*, 94

Bentley, Eric: and Wilde, Oscar, 13, 14; tragicomic theory, 19

Bergson, Henri: influence of *Creative Evolution*, 11; comic theory, 16; and *Lady*, 64, 69; *élan vital* in *Sleep*, 100, 101

Bible: influence on Fry, 11, 155; on *Boy*, 31, 32, 33; on *Firstborn*, 37–38; on *Phoenix*, 55; on *Lady*, 60, 71–72; on *Sleep*, 99–101

The Boy with a Cart: written, 10; influenced by *Bible*, 31, 32, 33; influenced by Eliot, T. S., *Murder*, 31, 34–36; influenced by *The Rock*, 31–32, 34; influenced by Williams, Charles, *Seed of Adam*, 35; influenced by Auden, W. H., 36; influenced by Bunyan, John, 36; and *Firstborn*, 38; and *Phoenix*, 51,

56; and *Thor*, 76; and *Sleep*, 108; and *Curtmantle*, 128, 136; imagery, 141–42

Brecht, Bertolt: contrariety in, 17; social criticism, 22; and Fry, 166

Brook, Peter: and *Venus*, 88

Brown, Pamela: and Fry, 11; and *Lady*, 59

Browne, E. Martin: and Mercury Theatre, 49; commissioned *Sleep*, 98

Browne, Sir Thomas: influence on Fry, 11, 156

Buchanan, Scott: "analogical matrix" and *Lady*, 74

Bunyan, John: influence on Fry, 7, 11, 36

Chapman, George: *Widow's Tears* and *Phoenix*, 51

Chaucer, Geoffrey: *Troilus and Criseyde* and *Lady*, 74; *Clerk's Tale* and *Dark*, 119

Chekhov, Anton: influence on Fry, 155

Coleridge, Samuel Taylor: theory of fancy, 142–43

"Comedy": and plays, 14–17; and *Sleep*, 102

Congreve, William: *Way of the World* produced by Fry, 11–12; and *Lady*, 60, 62